KETTLING THE UNIONS?
A guide to the 2016 Trade Union Act

Published with the support of

Public and
Commercial
Services Union

KETTLING THE UNIONS?
A guide to the 2016 Trade Union Act

By Alan Tuckman

with a foreword by Mark Serwotka

SPOKESMAN
Nottingham

First published in 2018 by
Spokesman Books
Russell House
Bulwell lane
Nottingham NG6 0BT
England

Phone 0115 9708318
Fax 0115 9420433
www.spokesmanbooks.com

A catalogue record is available from the British Library.

ISBN 978 085124 874 5

CONTENTS

FOREWORD

Mark Serwotka, General Secretary
Public and Commercial Services (PCS) Union

This very welcome book is intended to provide an analysis of the roots of the *Trade Union Act 2016*. Those roots lie in Thatcher's legislation of the 1980s and further back to the undermining of collective bargaining in UK industrial relations that developed in the 1970s, in the context of neoliberalism's rise to dominance.

The *Trade Union Act* was a transparent attempt to contain trade unions in the position they held before the turn of the 20th century. It has introduced draconian restrictions on the right to strike, and new restrictions covering balloting and picketing. It has also changed the rules on union political funds from the current 'opt-out' system to an 'opt-in' system, an anti-democratic attempt to reduce the ability of trade unions to fund not only political parties, but a wide range of other non-party political activities.

As well as aiming to be a guide to the 2016 *Trade Union Act* and its effect on the trade union movement, this book sets it in the context of decades of attacks on the rights of workers to organise by Conservative governments.

The weakening of the labour movement during the last quarter of the 20th Century has had a significant impact on the ability of working people to influence their standard of living and quality of life. The *Trade Union Act* is part of this bigger picture, and is the latest in a long line of attacks, implemented alongside other measures – cuts to public services, jobs, austerity – aimed at weakening organised labour and the rights of the most vulnerable in society.

We know now that the Conservative government intended to go much further, with new anti-trade union measures planned, after the 2017 general election. It was only the unexpected result of the general election – the success of the Labour party under Jeremy Corbyn and the failure of May to achieve a Tory majority in parliament – that stopped them. Now, potentially, there is a very different future possible, with a strong Labour party, led by Jeremy Corbyn and John McDonnell, whose stated aim is to restore trade union rights and collective bargaining: long held demands of our movement.

Collective bargaining is the most effective way of protecting workplace rights and ensuring decent pay. We know from experience that Conservative governments are intent on preventing ordinary workers – particularly those in the public sector – from organising collectively to fight back against the extreme attacks on their living standards, working conditions and pay.

Trade unions are the largest voluntary organisations in Britain, with 6.5 million members. If it wasn't for trade unions, collective bargaining and the right to strike, there would be no barrier to moving millions more workers – including public-sector workers – on to minimum-wage, zero-hour contracts.

However, the coverage of collective bargaining now stands at below 25% in the UK, down from 82% in 1979. As this book highlights, this decline has been shaped by anti-trade union laws over the last 30 years which inhibit trade union recruitment, activity, and bargaining power. Analysis of the UK economy over the past 30 years shows how the decline of collective bargaining coverage has coincided with the dramatic decrease in the proportion of GDP that goes to workers' pay, and the equally dramatic rise of profits and executive pay.

While these ideological restrictions were being implemented, new and emerging types of underemployment and insecure work increased dramatically, with almost 60% of new jobs created from 2010-15 in low-paid sectors of the economy. Around 1-in-5 employees (around 4.9 million people) earn less than the Living Wage and there are at least 1.4 million workers on zero-hours contracts (and potentially 1.3 million more not included in official figures).

Such a dramatic shift in the balance of power away from ordinary workers is further undermining the pay and conditions of every worker, exacerbating the growing gulf between wages and the cost of living, further increasing inequality and destroying long-established workplace rights introduced to protect employees from exploitation.

Recent polling by Ipsos Mori found nearly 80% of the public think "trade unions are essential to protect workers' interests", support that has been consistent for decades.

This book sets out how we got here, and argues that we must now recreate a movement with the political and social influence that enabled the former labour movement to achieve the major reductions in inequality during the middle decades of the 20th Century. A fairer and more sustainable future is possible, and I hope that this very timely book will act as a practical guide for trade unionists and also as an introduction to the subject for political activists and interested readers.

PREFACE

Oil on the Fire?

Brexit and Workers' Rights

At the time of the 1975 referendum on membership of the European Economic Community, the EEC, which later became the European Union, most trade unions and most of the left were opposed to membership of what was considered the 'rich man's club'. In 1971 the TUC conference passed a motion opposing membership in principle. By the time of the second referendum, in 2016, most trade unions and the TUC[1] favoured the continuation of UK membership. A central reason for this 'conversion', it seems, is the significant expansion of employment rights that has been achieved through the European Union.

From the founding of the Community by the original six countries in the 1950s, the principle of free movement of both capital and of labour has operated. These principles became embedded in the 1968 Directive which stated that:

'the right of freedom of movement, in order that it may be exercised, by objective standards, in freedom and dignity, requires that equality of treatment shall be ensured in fact and in law in respect of all matters relating to the actual pursuit of activities as employed persons and to eligibility for housing, and also that obstacles to the mobility of workers shall be eliminated, in particular as regards the worker's right to be joined by his family and the conditions for the integration of that family into the host country.'[2]

Migration has been central to economic development, and the rise of industry in the UK was dependent on it. In examining the condition of the working class in England in the 1840s, Frederick Engels was clear that this class was made up of a sizeable proportion of migrants from Ireland and their descendants. Escaping the impoverishment of Ireland as the effect of English colonialism, these migrants also experienced the worst conditions on arrival in England and Scotland.

'The rapid extension of English industry could not have taken place if England had not possessed in the numerous and impoverished population of Ireland a reserve at command. The Irish had nothing to lose at home, and much to gain in England ... It has been calculated that more than a million have already

9

immigrated, and not far from fifty thousand still come every year, nearly all of whom enter the industrial districts, especially the great cities, and there form the lowest class of the population.'[3]

Not only did the Irish form a sizeable proportion of workers in the mills of Manchester, but they also dug the canals, built the railways, the docks, and much of the new factory and housing stock which defined the new industrial cities.

Post-war economic recovery had also been built on the international movement of labour: in Germany on Turkish migrants working on the assembly lines of the motor industry; North African workers in France; and, of course, workers from the Commonwealth in the UK, from the Indian subcontinent for the declining textile industry, or from the Caribbean for the NHS and the public services, as well as the continued flow of those coming to work from Ireland.

While initially small scale, the possibility of short-term migration of labour was not lost on UK workers. With the election of Margaret Thatcher's government in 1979, and the beginnings of neoliberalism with a vengeance, traditional industries were decimated and a policy of de-industrialisation dominated. The potential for the free movement of skilled labour became embedded in popular culture with the television series *Auf Wiedersehen, Pet*, which told the story of a gang of construction workers who moved to Germany for work.

Reversals in political attitudes to the European Community began in the mid-80s with the publication of the *Single European Act*, which proposed the completion of the internal market by 1992. What appeared as the fruition of the neoliberal, free-market project was signed by Thatcher in 1987. However, this was also to be the transition point after which Thatcher moved to a more antagonistic position towards the EC and the unions moved towards it.

The shift by the unions can be dated from the speech delivered by Jacques Delors, President of the EEC at the time, at the TUC Congress of 1988. His speech pointed to the 'mechanisms of social solidarity, of protection of the weakest, and of collective bargaining', which characterised the strength of European post-war economies. Integral to the completion of the internal market, Delors' proposed a model of Social Europe:

'Firstly, measures adopted to complete the large market should not diminish the level of social protection already achieved in the member states. Second, the internal market should be designed to benefit each and every citizen of the

10

community. It is therefore necessary to improve workers' living and working conditions, and to provide better protection for their health and safety at work. Third, the measures to be taken will concern the area of collective bargaining and legislation.'[4]

Within days, Margaret Thatcher was addressing the College of Europe, in what became known as her Bruges speech, perhaps the founding statement of 'official' Conservative Euro-scepticism. Challenging the views expressed by Delors, she argued that:

> 'we certainly do not need new regulations which raise the cost of employment and make Europe's labour market less flexible and less competitive with overseas suppliers. If we are to have a European Company Statute, it should contain the minimum regulations. And certainly we in Britain would fight attempts to introduce collectivism and corporatism at the European level– although what people wish to do in their own countries is a matter for them.'[5]

The extension of the social model became embedded in 1993 with the signing of the *Maastricht Treaty* which recognised the fulfilment of the internal market. The UK government's opposition came with their refusal to sign the *Social Chapter* of the Treaty. Until the *Chapter* was signed by the incoming Blair government in 1997, the UK remained outside of new regulations on working conditions, health and safety, discrimination, gender equality, as well as on information and consultation of employees.

Increasingly, the unions found the EU and the European Court of Justice (ECJ) to be useful vehicles for defending workers' rights, in the context where the Thatcher government had introduced a raft of anti-trade union legislation. This came alongside a decline in employment conditions driven by the increased fetishization of markets: the raft of privatisation and outsourcing initiated by the Thatcher Government had entailed a change in employer for many. This meant declining conditions for often low paid workers as they moved into employment by contractors and agencies. This resulted in a deliberate 'drive to the bottom' in terms and conditions for workers employed by companies squeezing costs in competing for these contracts. Unions could challenge such developments using *The Acquired Rights Directive* of 1977, arguing that it ought to be enacted into UK legislation. This came about in 1981 with the *Transfer of Undertakings (Protection of Employment)* – or TUPE – Regulations. However, the neoliberal hostility towards regulations which attempt to directly protect the terms and conditions of workers can be seen in the introduction to a government review into the TUPE regulation, in which the point is made that regulations should 'ensure they provide the flexibility that employers need to grow and compete effectively.'[6]

The incorporation of European Directives into UK legislation quickly created grounds for the popular press to attack what they presented as European 'bureaucracy' and 'mindless regulation'. Stories about the alleged 'mindlessness' of health and safety regulation became the bread-and-butter of *The Sun* newspaper. Health and Safety Officers took their place in the pantheon of folk devils which had been occupied by shop stewards a decade or more before. This vilification continued even when the *Working Time Directive*, whose objective was to try to reduce working time to a 35-hour week, was watered down in UK legislation, allowing for an opt-out from the maximum 48-hour working week.

The biggest challenge to free movement developed with the expansion of the EU in 2004, with the accession of eight Eastern European states. Between 2004 and 2006 an estimated 410,00 workers from accession countries, predominantly from Poland, entered the UK economy.[7] The collapse of the economies of Eastern Europe, and the wholesale privatisation grab, threw millions of highly skilled and disciplined workers into unemployment. These workers became a reserve army to be recruited by Western capital, which had undergone a major restructuring since the crisis of the 1970s. UK employers actively sought workers to fill vacant jobs in new areas of expansion, such as warehousing, or which were vacant because domestic workers refused to fill them. About half the workers moving from other EU countries had already secured jobs in the UK.[8] Agencies recruited in Eastern Europe to fill vacant jobs in the new sweatshops, such as at Sports Direct, where they would work long hours under draconian discipline. Industries such as agriculture, food processing, and hospitality, which had always been dependent on seasonal labour, began to look further afield to fill vacancies. The long-term decline in vocational education in the UK, exacerbated by underfunding since the rise of Thatcher, meant migration was needed to fill the skills void. In the mythology peddled by sections of the press and anti-immigrant politicians, the UK was 'flooded' by Polish plumbers.

A project in the East Midlands, based around three case studies, tried to highlight good practice in atypical employment of migrant workers from Eastern Europe. A bus company sought drivers willing to work long and unsocial hours. They had first recruited from Malta and then from Portugal – drivers who, management considered, had become increasingly 'unreliable' – before sending recruiters to Eastern Europe. A furniture factory sought recruits from Poland and Latvia after experiencing high labour turnover. This turnover, along with a deterioration in the company's reputation in the local labour market, followed the introduction of a new production system and the scrapping of an established bonus payment system. The third case, of the Fire and Rescue Service, was in some ways most distant from the stereotypical experience but closest to the economic driver of much migrant recruitment. The employment of part-time – retained – firefighters, the normal pattern outside of cities, has been constrained by the conversion of country villages into 'commuter belt' territory. Eastern European migrants replaced seasonal workers, who might in the past have been drawn from local communities. However, the very mobility and long hours expected of the migrant workers prohibited their filling the gap in the ranks of retained firefighters. Only one was recruited, who managed to fulfil these obligations alongside childcare, rather than factory work. The Service had, however, found the need to recruit workers from the Eastern European community to carry out the fire prevention work in the food processing plants, as they were concerned about the robust and accurate translation of fire procedures.[9]

EU Directives and decisions of the European Court of Justice on free movement have not always appeared positive for trade unions. To cover workers sent temporarily to another EU state the Commission passed the *Posted Workers Directive* in 1996. Judges at the ECJ ruled that this allowed certain workers to be employed under their home country terms and conditions, not those of the country to which they are posted. In 2009 a strike of construction workers broke out at the Lindsey Oil Refinery in North Lincolnshire. The Italian construction company engaged for work on the site had brought in an Italian workforce, and billeted them on a ferry off Grimsby, rather than employ the local workforce. The suspicion that sparked the strike was that this was to undercut the terms and conditions of local workers.[10]

Brexit raises numerous questions concerning the future of migration, free movement and workers' rights. Despite frequently expressing her concern for employment rights, and her determination to preserve them, Theresa May remains unconvincing. Even senior Conservatives seem sceptical. In the debate on the *European Union (Withdrawal) Bill*, Ken Clarke, a Minister in the Thatcher, Major and Cameron governments, commented that:

'Heaven forfend that my party should swing to the right at any time in its long and distinguished history, but there are members of the present Government who are not excessively fond of lizards and bats, or workers' rights. We would all be reassured if he undertook to put in the Bill a reduced level of powers.'[11]

A Labour amendment to the Bill, which would have included guarantees that workers' rights derived from EU membership would be maintained after Brexit, was defeated by 12 votes after opposition from the Conservatives who considered such a measure 'unnecessary'. Given the fixation with the reduction of regulation it would also seem unlikely that measures derived from the *Working Time Directive* will remain after ministerial scrutiny under a Conservative government. Given also the disdain of the popular press and of neoliberal ideologues, who hold to the view that the very notion of health and safety has become synonymous with absurd state interference and regulation of the free market, it would be surprising if all protections remained intact.

The issue of mobility, or alternatively the right to stay put, is dependent on the definition of citizenship and citizens' rights following 2019. Also, given the historic relations between Ireland and the UK, the significance of the border cannot be underestimated. Most of the discussion has been concerned with the flow of goods and little to do with that of people. An 'open border' would clearly be a backdoor into, and out of, the EU labour market post-Brexit. However, in the past the flow of labour was essentially from Ireland to the UK. If the prognosis is correct, that post-Brexit employment conditions in the UK will enter a downward spiral in competition with the sweatshop economies for jobs and investment, then the border might become a new exit for UK workers seeking the thriving and more secure conditions of the EU.

Notes:

1. See e.g. TUC, UK Employment Rights and the EU (2016); available from https://www.tuc.org.uk/node/124569
2. *Regulation (EEC) No. 1612/68 and Directive on Freedom of Movement for Workers in the Community*, Official Journal of the European Economic Communities of 19 October 1968, p. 10
3. Friedrich Engels, 'The Condition of the Working-Class in England', in *Karl Marx Frederick Engels: Collected Works, Volume 4 1844-1845*, p. 389
4. *1992: The Social Dimension*, address by Jacques Delors, President of The Commission of the European Communities, Trade Union Congress, Bournemouth 8 September 1988
5. Speech to the College of Europe ('The Bruges Speech'), 20 September 1988, available at http://www.margaretthatcher.org/document/107332
6. Cited in Roger Jeary, *TUPE: From Protection of Employees, to Promises for Employers* (6 March 2013); available from http://www.ier.org.uk/blog/tupe-protection-employees-promises-employers
7. Based on application for National Insurance Numbers required for employment in the UK, *Accession Monitoring Report*, May 2004 – June 2006, Home Office
8. See the *Migration Statistics Quarterly Report* statistical bulletins, available from the Office of National Statistics (https://www.ons.gov.uk/)
9. Alan Tuckman and Lynette Harris, *The Employment of Migrant Labour in the East Midlands*, Acas Research Papers (London: ACAS, 2009)
10. See Acas, *Report of an Inquiry into the Circumstances Surrounding the Lindsey Oil Refinery Dispute* (London: Advisory, Conciliation and Arbitration Service, 2009). 16 February 2009
11. Kenneth Clarke at https://hansard.parliament.uk/commons/2017-11-15/debates/7A700C0E-8BA2-4EEC-B53D-997028C06900/EuropeanUnion(Withdrawal)Bill

Introduction

On the 7th May 2015 the Conservatives, with less than 37 per-cent of the vote and a 12-seat majority in the House of Commons, set about forming a government under David Cameron. This surprise result followed the collapse of the Liberal Democrats in England, and the Labour Party in Scotland. The Conservatives now governed alone, allowing them to attempt to complete some unfinished business from the Major government: the further containment of trade unions.

The Conservatives' manifesto of 2015, argued – ominously for the unions – that:

> 'Strikes should only ever be the result of a clear, positive decision based on a ballot in which at least half the workforce has voted. This turnout threshold will be an important and fair step to rebalance the interests of employers, employees, the public and the rights of trade unions. We will, in addition, tackle the disproportionate impact of strikes in essential public services by introducing a tougher threshold in health, education, fire and transport. Industrial action in these essential services would require the support of at least 40 per cent of all those entitled to take part in strike ballots - as well as a majority of those who actually turn out to vote. We will also repeal nonsensical restrictions banning employers from hiring agency staff to provide essential cover during strikes; and ensure strikes cannot be called on the basis of ballots conducted years before.'[1]

Clearly, their ambitions were much broader than just attacking the use of the strike weapon. With further restrictions on picketing during strikes, attacks on trade union funding and the ability of employee representatives to carry out their role, Cameron's Conservatives aimed to mount a serious and significant attack. The manifesto further proposed that if elected a Conservative government would:

> 'tackle intimidation of non-striking workers; legislate to ensure trade unions use a transparent opt-in process for union subscriptions; tighten the rules around taxpayer-funded paid 'facility' time' for union representatives; and reform the role of the Certification Officer.'[2]

In July, only weeks after their election victory, the *Trade Union Bill* was published that incorporated the manifesto commitments. The removal of the ban on strike breaking agencies was not in the Bill as it required only a change of existing regulation. However, a further measure which hadn't

16

appeared in the manifesto was added to the Bill. The new Conservative government, flushed by its unexpected electoral victory, now proposed to limit trade union funding of the Labour Party and other political campaigns and causes.

An early test of the new government, the Bill found opposition in its transition through Parliament, including from some Conservative peers who were critical of the attack on another party's funding. Opposition to the Bill also came from all opposition parties, most notably from the newly expanded contingent of Scottish Nationalists in the Commons. The government was forced into making some concessions, including limiting the impact on political funding, as well as establishing an inquiry into e-balloting, before the Bill got Royal Assent in May 2016. The main sections of the Bill came into law as the *Trade Union Act* in March 2017. While the concessions drawn in the transit through Parliament were important, the major test of the measures in the Act will be the reaction of the unions, workers and, as significantly, employers, the police, and the judiciary. Will workers and their unions be willing to fight injustice in the workplace and the wider economy, on picket lines and elsewhere despite the constraints of the law? If they are, how will the new laws be implemented against them?

While posing new legal challenges to action by trade unions, the proposals in the 2016 Act form part of a deliberate attack on the very nature and position of trade unions in contemporary British society. As well as strengthening the legal cordon around the activities of trade unions, this was an ideological assault. For some of their critics the unions had gained too much power, particularly to withdraw labour. Others argued that because of enlightened employers, and improved conditions, trade unions had become redundant. Earlier proposals for trade union reform, from the 1960s onwards, tended to rest on arguments about relative power: not only was Britain particularly strike prone, what became known as the 'British disease', but also that union leaders had gained access to government and the institutions of power. This was the rallying cry of the Thatcher government against the unions in a series of measures to contain the unions throughout the 1980s.

Pure anti-trade unionism, rooted in the attitude that workers ought to know their place, accept their lot, and of course be deferential to their betters clearly informs much of this attack. Challenges to this view can be characterised as 'the servant problem', neatly summarised by E.P. Thompson in his analysis of letters written to *The Times*.[3] Industrial action by workers required their 'betters' to use candles to light their homes and had driven them to voice their complaints through the letters page of *The Times*. The target of the 'servant problem' has moved from the miners to transport workers and other 'public servants'. Industrial action by such groups means they are not at the beck and call of their masters. The housemaid who didn't answer the bell is replaced by the worker responsible for the light not coming on at the flick of a switch, along with the railway guard whose strike means the trains fail to run.

Early industrial authority drew from the agricultural estates, a direct and very local form of master and servant relationship. In exchange for deference, the worker was rewarded with paternal care and protection, which often included housing and welfare provision for young and old. New model employers, such as Titus Salt who established his mill town of Saltair in the West Riding of Yorkshire, or later the Cadbury family with Bournville in Birmingham, provided not just housing but also wide social provision and lifetime employment from one generation to the next. Perhaps the pinnacle of this tradition can be seen with Henry Ford in the USA in the early 20th century. High wages and welfare came with the expectation of obedience to authority. Ford's strict rules of conduct within and outside work were enforced by the threat of dismissal if there was any transgression. Independent action, or organisation, by the workforce was unthinkable to such autocrats.

Forceful challenges by organised workers sealed the fate of two previous attempts at containing the trade unions, the first by Wilson's Labour government in the form of *In Place of Strife* in 1969, and the Heath Conservative government's in 1971 with the *Industrial Relations Act*. Both collapsed through union opposition, the latter through union 'disobedience'. Thatcher learnt lessons from this experience, opting to increase the containment of the unions in a 'legal kettling' manoeuvre. Since 1979 the trade unions have increasingly been surrounded by regulations governing their action; this of course applies particularly to all aspects of industrial action but also to their own trade union rules and government. Progressively – or perhaps more accurately regressively – and like the police 'kettling' of demonstrators, this regulation has become increasingly tightened. So, while using the main weapon they have at their disposal to challenge employers, trade unionists have found themselves increasingly contained within a 'policing' cordon, a cordon which tightens until there is no longer room for movement.

The containment of trade unions was, of course, only one of the elements within the broader 'Thatcher project', although a major one. The challenge to organised labour was staged to enable, and ease, the shift in policy from interventionism to free market liberalism. Away went Keynesian economic management, and in came the economics of the 'new right' or neoliberalism as it was later dubbed (see Box 1.13 and Section 1 for a fuller discussion of neoliberalism). First came 'monetarism' to shrink state spending and then the sell-off of public goods to the private sector as 'state' shifted to 'free market'. Perhaps ironically for trade unions, as the neoliberal project trumpeted a 'free' and deregulated economy, they were to be more and more tightly controlled. The limited role of the state in employment relations which characterised the first three-quarters of the twentieth century, through a system termed 'voluntarism', was replaced by an increasing legal cordon. Mutual trust and the establishment of rules through collective bargaining – the cornerstones of voluntarism – were replaced with the unilateral imposition of managerial authority: a move to 'master and servant'.

The watchwords of the new employment relations became 'management's right to manage' as the interests of business, and particularly of big business, were presented as the interests of society as a whole. With the increasing disappearance of manufacturing industry, through bankruptcy or a move eastward to the developing economies of Asia, these interests were increasingly those of the banks and finance capital. The local, paternalistic, company which 'looked after their workers' – as long as they were compliant – was swallowed up or disappeared in a wave of capital rationalisation and consolidation in the wake of periodic economic crises.

Significant changes in employment practices also happened within this restructuring, that moved away from the days of 'master and servant'. Now there were no longer any obligations from the 'masters' to their 'servants', the relationship was no longer one of 'paternalism'. Employers absolved themselves of any ethical responsibility for the welfare provision of their employees. Pension schemes disappeared along with any equation of the wage with the cost of living. Overtime payments at extra rate, to compensate for working anti-social hours, also went with any concern for life outside the workplace. The notion of a 'work-life balance' only appeared in management rhetoric, and began to disappear from the experiences of the employees.

'Human resources', management jargon to mystify the disembodied labour they purchase, came under the same scrutiny as other 'cost inputs' to the business. Changes in management ideology, including the fashion for 'just-in-time' systems, meant that human labour could be whittled down to a minimum, like other raw materials. First, in a wave of delayering with consequent redundancies, organisations were to cut down to core-business. What followed was casualisation and outsourcing of labour. Security of employment has been drastically diminished in a drive for flexibility, resulting in a precarious labour market and the rise of zero-hour contracts.

While there were some heroic struggles, the unions were increasingly impotent. This was partly because of the haemorrhaging of membership in their traditional powerbases of the manufacturing industries. Members were lost through closures rather than by resignation from the union. But how could unions survive without recruiting replacements for the membership they were losing, not least because of declining income? Challenges to voluntarism, which had been the central ideology of trade unionism, as well as the employment policy plank for post-war governments, mounted steadily. Some began to accept that a shift to the free market, with the breakdown of the collectivism of trade unionism, was an inevitability that had to be accommodated to. Some began to argue that, to stay viable, unions needed to accept and adapt to the 'new realities' of Thatcher's Britain. Trade unions, it was argued, were themselves businesses selling their services. Influential advocacy of this position came in a Fabian Society pamphlet, written by Philip Bassett and Alan Cave, the Industrial Editor of *The Times* and an ex-trade union officer. Basset and Cave, in an approach which appealed to some trade unions at the time, asked a series of questions concerning the very viability of trade unions in this 'new reality':

> 'In the way the unions work, in the way they are organised, in their role and direction, how far are Britain's unions capable of embracing the new individualism as it appears at work, among employers and employees?'[4]

And to what extent were the unions capable of shifting to what the authors saw as the inevitable ascendency of market forces?

> 'How far are they willing to do so? Can trade unions ever be capable of a more individualistic focus, or are they so inherently collectivist that they run the risk of becoming increasingly inappropriate to the individually-based political, social and occupational flexibility of the 1990s and beyond?'

Failure to accommodate to the changing times raised the very viability of trade unions in this new reality:

There is an argument that the role of the unions is past - that the historical moment of collectivism is over, made unnecessary by social improvement, and largely and repeatedly rejected by employees, as made manifest by the trade unions continually falling membership rolls.

In the ethos of Thatcherism, and like many organisations in the era of neoliberalism, the unions ought to consider themselves as the sellers of services to employers and employees, and that: '[t]he traditional core product from unions is support for collective bargaining in order to provide collective benefits for their members.'[5] Such a 'business model' had been adopted by some unions willing to 'sell' agreements to employers, which included such features as 'no strike' clauses, sometimes on greenfield sites and before a workforce had been recruited.[6] This poaching of membership could, of course, be the cause of further complication and tension in an inter-union dispute, as well as aggravate the dispute with the employer.

In 1986, a year after the long-running miners' strike came to an end, print workers in London began industrial action against News International, the newspaper group owned by Rupert Murdoch. The dispute, arising from the move from Fleet Street to Wapping, was effectively a lock-out rather than a strike. As well as the move to new premises and the adoption of new technology, one of Murdoch's central objectives was the breaking of the print unions, along with the organisation of journalists and others in the production and distribution of newspapers. Prior to the move to Wapping, News International signed a secret recognition agreement with a far more compliant union, the Electrical, Electronic & Telecommunication & Plumbing Union (EETPU). The industrial action sparked by News International also allowed management to dismiss strikers under the recent Thatcher government employment legislation. Strikers were replaced by the EEPTU 'members' who crossed the picket line at the new Wapping plant.[7]

The proposals by Cave and Bassett and their 'new realism' went further than just advocating the sale of collective bargaining services to employers. In examining possible directions to ensure their future, they argued that trade unions should become 'private service' providers comparable to 'private medical bodies':

'Like the unions, the private medical bodies provide a range of services for an important area of their purchasing members' lives - in the unions' case, employment, and the private medical providers' case, health. Like the unions,

21

the private medical bodies provide benefits in their operational areas which supplement those provided by the state. And like the unions, the private medical bodies compete strongly with one another for members.'[8]

We have seen, as had they, what the competition for membership meant at Wapping, but they saw their prescription as a move away from class mobilisation and strikes towards membership as passive consumers of services. The comparable organisation to which the trade unions should model themselves, they suggested, were the automobile breakdown services.

> 'In directly offering to their members more overtly consumerist services, unions have made moves which prompt obvious and genuine parallels with such organisations as the AA [Automobile Association]. Indeed, many are now in direct and open competition with the AA selling insurance as the AA sells insurance, for example. Many unions have drawn the parallels even closer, by moving openly into the car breakdown market, offering their members discount schemes with more minor players in the AA's still-core market.'[9]

The trade unions were presented as the providers of insurance, holidays, as well as legal services to whoever decides on membership. Cave and Bassett present their argument very much as sympathisers on a rearguard action to save trade unions from what could be the inevitable march of history, or perhaps more accurately the march of the market economy. Further tightening of Thatcher's trade union laws, particularly the outlawing of the closed shop, and an increased dismissal of collective bargaining by employers, relegated this approach to oblivion even amongst the most compliant unions.

While there is a high degree of class antagonism to trade unionism, which we can represent as that of 'master and servant', a rather more sophisticated approach is embedded within neoliberalism. Neoliberalism has a fundamental opposition to collective bargaining. Notions of any 'collective' are an anathema with any bargaining on the market between 'individuals,' even if these 'individuals' are sometimes global corporations, with a purely legal status as an 'individual' through incorporation. What Cave and Bassett considered the union's 'core business', would be accepted by neoliberal thinkers as organisations providing service provision as long as membership of such organisations was voluntary. The services that some neoliberals anticipate unions providing would throw trade unions back to their origins long before the welfare state. Early trade unions were formally 'friendly societies' and provided benefits for sickness, accidents, death, and other eventualities. The desired destination appears not in the future but in past roles of trade unions. With the rolling-back of the welfare state, the destination appears one resting firmly in the 19th century where benefits flow not from the state but from the mutuality of the workers.

Such a claim for a 19th century vision is not just based around the possible provision of welfare services but also on another fixation of neoliberalism, the legal status of trade unions. A central argument which runs through neoliberal ideas, and a bugbear for Thatcher's guru Frederic Hayek, were the immunities given to trade unions against civil prosecution when action is taken in furtherance of a trade dispute.[10] These immunities were granted in the *Trade Union Act of 1906* and Hayek long campaigned for its repeal. The 1906 Act did not put trade unions above the law, as Hayek claimed, but gave them limited dispensation in civil law during industrial action or, as the Act puts it, 'trade disputes'. This only applies to civil law, to acts of tort, and has no impact on any actions that might be deemed against criminal law. The 1906 Act was a rather crude attempt to accommodate the trade unions at the time within the UK system of common law, largely established by judges. While an immediate reaction to the rulings of some judges, this accommodation had none of the surrealism of establishing capitalist enterprises as 'corporations', allowing them to take on the legal status of individuals. 'Incorporation' is unquestioned by neoliberals who, in fact, place this centrally in their argument concerning the equality of 'individuals' engaging on the free market. Hayek was calling for a return to the legal position of trade unions before 1906. The 1906 Act, while giving immunity to trade unions during a trade dispute, did not define what constituted such a dispute. While not totally abolishing immunity from civil wrong, the Thatcher reforms increasingly limited what might be considered a legitimate trade dispute to qualify for this immunity. Perhaps with little thought of gaining a majority in the 2015 election, the framers of Cameron's manifesto proposed to take further steps towards Hayek's objective of abolishing these trade union immunities. Since the Thatcher legislation of the 1980s this objective had been pursued, not as tried in 1971 with the *Industrial Relations Act*, but as a slow war of attrition through 'salami slicing', or as increasing constraint on trade union action.

The overall thrust of Conservative trade union policy has been an attempt to return to the conditions of Victorian Britain. This attempt to recapture past glories is evident in some of the arguments around Brexit, the issue that dominated politics in the UK through the period when the

Bill was under consideration, and gave it a particular turbulence. As well as its promise to tighten the laws governing the action of trade unions, the Conservative manifesto for the 2015 election promised that:

> 'after the election, we will negotiate a new settlement for Britain in Europe, and then ask the British people whether they want to stay in the EU on this reformed basis or leave. David Cameron has committed that he will only lead a government that offers an in-out referendum. We will hold that in-out referendum before the end of 2017 and respect the outcome.'[11]

A criticism of the EU which came from neoliberals was that, as the UK was moving towards a 'free market' and disentangling regulation, the opposite was happening in Europe. The European 'common market' added a social dimension, that of social protection (see Box 1). The European Community and the European Union that followed, increasingly concerned itself with working conditions and access to corporate decision making. Some of the measures, such as the Working Time Directive, were introduced under the auspices of health and safety regulation, a term which itself became used by critics as synonmous with bureacratic regulation.

The Brexit referendum was held on 23rd June 2016, less than six weeks after the *Trade Union Act* came into UK law, with a victory for those wanting to leave the European Union. This result led to the resignation of David Cameron, who was replaced as Prime Minister by Theresa May. While the government promised that Brexit would not be detrimental to employment rights there were certainly concerns that it would lead to an undermining of protections offered by EU membership. While the succession in the Conservative Party seemed relatively quick and painless, with potential candidates for the premiership falling by the wayside, changes in the Labour leadership proved more rancorous.

With little initial expectation of success, Jeremy Corbyn won the leadership of the Labour Party. Within a year the Parliamentary party had passed a vote of no confidence, and Corbyn faced a challenge for the leadership. While winning against the insurgents, Corbyn's position still appeared weak. In the circumstances, and contrary to previous promises, Theresa May called a snap general election to increase the slim working majority of fifteen seats she inherited from the 2015 election. Boosting her majority, based on her 'strong and stable leadership', she argued that a Conservative government with a substantial majority would give weight to her Brexit negotiations with the EU.

Box 1: *Employment Regulation arising from EU Directives*

Working Time Regulations 1998
*   maximum weekly working hours
*   daily and weekly rest breaks
*   holiday entitlement
*   UK opt-out of the 48-hour working week

Equality Act 2010
*   discrimination based on sex, race, caste, religion or belief, disability, age, sexual orientation and gender reassignment, marriage and civil partnerships
*   maternity and paternity rights

Agency Workers Regulations 2010
*   equal treatment of agency workers with 'comparable' permanent workers

The Part-Time Employees (Prevention of Less Favourable Treatment) Regulations 2000

The Fixed-Term Employees (Prevention of Less Favourable Treatment) Regulations 2002

Employee Consultation
*   European Works Council Directive and Information and Consultation of Employees Directive

TUPE (Transfer of Undertakings Protection of Employment) Regulations
*   Employee rights when employment changes due to take-over.

During the election campaign, as May's popularity went into freefall, Corbyn's fortunes climbed. In the final results, rather than an increase, May lost the Conservative majority and needed to gain an agreement from the Democratic Unionist Party to remain in power, while Labour gained 32 seats which secured Corbyn's position. While not in any way key to their electoral fortunes, their 2017 manifesto promised that a Labour government would:

> 'Repeal the Trade Union Act and roll out sectoral collective bargaining because the most effective way to maintain good rights at work is collectively through a union. Guarantee trade unions a right to access workplaces so that unions can speak to members and potential members.'[12]

They also promised to ban zero hours contracts, raise the minimum wage, and end the public-sector wage cap introduced by the Cameron government as part of their austerity measures.

The focus of this book is the *Trade Union Act* of 2016. To understand it requires more than a clause by clause examination which is given in Section 3. The broader context is vital. Firstly, the Act itself technically amends existing legislation, the *Trade Union and Labour Relations Act* (TULR) 1992, which brought together the series of measures introduced by the Thatcher Government to control and contain the trade unions. This legislation, introduced in a series of Parliamentary Acts after 1980 and consolidated in TULR, placed a cordon around trade unions. Section Two examines the trade union reforms since the 1960s, with Labour's *In Place of Strife*, the Conservative's *Industrial Relations Act*, the minor respite and consolidation of trade union and employment rights in the 1970s, followed by the reforms introduced by Thatcher and Major in the 1980s and 1990s.

Also of great significance is the clash of ideas concerning the nature and role of trade unions in society. The first section examines two competing views of trade unions and labour relations: 'voluntarism', rooted in the changes at the turn of the 20th century and becoming the orthodoxy within government policy, with prescriptions for joint regulation of employment through collective bargaining; and Thatcherism, the initial UK variant of neoliberalism, which challenged the policies of state intervention and attacked trade unions as anti-market, with 'monopoly power' over the provision of labour. While the proposers of the 2016 Act presented it as a measure to modernise the trade unions, the measure was built on the legislative and ideological foundations of earlier onslaughts, which sought to send trade unions into the 19th and not the 21st century.

Notes:

1. *Conservative Manifesto* 2015, p.18
2. Ibid, p. 19
3. Thompson, E. P. 'Sir, Writing by Candlelight...' *New Society* 24 (1970), reprinted in his collection of articles under the same title published by Merlin Press, 1980
4. Philip Bassett and Alan Cave, *All for One: The Future of the Unions* (London: The Fabian Society, 1993), p.1
5. Ibid, p.3
6. See Philip Bassett's earlier work, *Strike Free: New Industrial Relations in Britain* (Macmillan Publishers Limited, 1986)
7. For more detail on the Wapping dispute see John Lang and Graham Dodkins, *Bad News: The Wapping Dispute* (Spokesman Books, 2011), and also see www.wapping-dispute.org.uk
8. Philip Bassett and Alan Cave, *All for One: The Future of the Unions* p.18
9. Ibid, p.19
10. See e.g. F.A. Hayek, *A Tiger By the Tail* (London: Institute of Economic Affairs, 1972); "Trade Union Immunity Under the Law" (Hayek Letter) [Revoke Privileges Granted By Trade Disputes Act, 1906] (1977); available from http://www.margaretthatcher.org/document/114630. See also Hanson, ibid. These grossly exaggerate the immunities of trade union, claiming it places them above the law during trade disputes
11. Conservative Party, The Conservative Party Manifesto 2015 (Conservative Party, 2015), p. 72
12. Labour Party, *For the Many Not the Few* (2017), p.47

Chapter 1:
The Trade Union Problem

The Emerging Problem

Trade unions have their roots in the emergence of industrial capitalism, and their history shapes the working class movement, its traditions and actions. While there were certainly collective organisations established by skilled workers in medieval societies, guilds of craft workers for example, the roots of trade unionism can be found in workers' collective reactions to pay and conditions in an increasingly cash – and wage – economy: the mills, mines, factories and workshops of the eighteenth and nineteenth century. Without a formal voice of protest to employers or the state, working people would take to the streets, in what Hobsbawm referred to as 'collective bargaining by riot.'[1] The emergence of formal trade union organisations was far from clear or straightforward, but was a heroic struggle for improvement through the autonomous organisation of working people. Trade union traditions are rooted in these struggles: of Luddites (see Box 1.1), not the mindless machine breakers of their reputation but challengers of mechanisation being used to undermine employment of skilled workers; of Dorset agricultural workers, the Tolpuddle Martyrs (Box 1.2), deported to Australia for taking an oath promising solidarity. The roots of unions also rest in the bargaining by – often independent – craft and skilled workers, with merchants and nascent capitalist entrepreneurs, over the rate for the job in local labour markets. The new trade unions were drawn into both conflict and cooperation with emergent capitalism. The unions always reflect a contradiction, one side organising the incorporation of the sale of labour power within capitalism and the other mobilising opposition to its fundamental drive to cheapen that very commodity.

The strength of workers' organisation allows some control of work and working conditions, control over the expenditure of labour power which is contested by management wanting to make the most of 'their human resource'. The boundaries of this workplace control shift with the relative strength of labour and capital, what the US economist Carter Goodrich argued was a shifting and contested 'frontier of control'[2]: organised labour's job protection and safer working might, for capital, represent a restrictive labour practice. This struggle is reflected within the legal and regulatory framework of work and employment relations. In times of

Box 1.1: *Luddites*

The Luddites were a movement of early 19th century textile workers protesting the introduction of machinery. Their opposition rested not only on the use of machines – mechanical frames – to replace their skilled labour with cheaper, less skilled workers, but also in the decline in quality of goods that this would bring. In a period of restriction, in the wake of the French Revolution and Napoleonic wars, the Luddites were the 'secret army' of the legendary Ned Ludd. Their tactic was the smashing of the machines which were undermining their living. To combat this, not only were large number of troops deployed to key areas such as Nottinghamshire and Yorkshire, but also Parliament introduced the Frame Breaking Act in 1812 which made machine breaking a capital offence.

relative strength organised workers may gain not just rights for trade union organisation itself but also some regulation of health and safety, on working hours, and on conditions more generally. A shift towards capital brings not just relaxation of regulation but also the tightening of control over trade unions. Crudely, we might see the period up to the turn of the 20th century as not just one of the rise of organised labour but also its incorporation into political society. From earlier craft organisation, this period not only culminated in growing organisation of new sections of workers into industrial and general unions, but also legitimating the role of unions and their activity in the *Trade Union Act* of 1906. Recession and unemployment in the 1920s and 1930s, as well as the aftermath of the General Strike in 1926, heralded a shift in the 'frontier of control' towards the interests of capital. Wartime economy, and post-war full employment and growth, once again enhanced the capacity of organised labour to gain concessions, peaking in the 1970s. The mid-1970s are often presented as a period of 'union power', with a phase of sympathetic employment legislation from the Labour Government as well as a high point of strike action. The strikes and legislation were seen as major problems for capital in limiting their capacity to fully exploit the labour power they were employing. The latest phase, which is the main concern of this book, represents the shift back to almost unilateral managerial prerogative – the absolute 'right to manage' – which has occurred since the 1980s. 'Thatcherism' came to represent changes which romanticised the free market economy and the individual entrepreneur in wealth creation. All this in practice masked the shift towards the economic dominance of global capitalism, with financial institutions squeezing out small scale and local capital. This basic economic shift was also the backdrop for a major attack on organised labour.

There was some rehearsal in the late 1960s and early 1970s, with Barbara Castle's white paper, *In Place of Strife*, or more substantially the Heath governments early promotion of neoliberalism – that 'lame duck' industries would be allowed to fail – which introduced control of trade unions through the *Industrial Relations Act* 1971. But the sustained attack on trade unions and shift in the 'frontier of control' came with the Thatcher governments of the 1980s. Section Two considers this containment of the trade unions, the 'Thatcher reforms', and Section Three the culmination of this in the *Trade Union Act 2016* which directly builds on these. But these changes are often presented as reforms which 'modernise' the trade unions, not least by members of the Cameron government in proposing the 2016 Act.

It is important not just to examine the regulations, controls, and enactments, but also to explore the ideological foundations on which these are built. While the promotors of these reforms, like the proposers of the 2016 Act, might present them as modernisation, or as pragmatic responses to the power of trade unions (as did the Thatcher government) the measures are deeply rooted in the ideology of market liberalism – or neoliberalism. This, in itself, reflects the interests of a particular section of capitalism, principally global finance.

The remainder of this section, while considering the establishment of trade unions and the ethos of their incorporation into British political society, also discusses the ideology of neoliberalism (see Box 1.13).

Box 1.2: *The Tolpuddle Martyrs*

In 1834 six Dorset farm labourers were prosecuted for taking an "illegal oath." Their crime was to protest to their employers who had cut their, already small, wage. Following their sentence to seven year's transportation to Australia there were massive protests and an 800,000-signature petition sent to Parliament. While later pardoned, only one of the martyrs returned to England. There is an annual festival in Dorset to commemorate the Tolpuddle martyrs.

The discussion of trade unions is rooted in competing sets of ideas and traditions. The shifts in policy reflecting the changing 'frontier of control' between employers and workers are also reflections of the shifts between 'common sense' ideas of workers and trade unions, and of capital, employers and the market. The ethos of trade unionism is broadly one of collectivism and mutual support, built around the demands of work, reinforced by the reason for the sale of labour being ultimately the need to purchase things needed to support life on the market. In contrast, the interests of capitalism have been expressed in terms of competition between individuals, in which there is a survival of the fittest in the market. Society itself is presented as the result of a contract – the 'social contract' – between these individuals escaping from a state of nature. Any progress is seen as the expression of individual talent or capacity – of individual entrepreneurship – rather than a collective effort. While these ideas were increasingly eclipsed, especially after periodic economic crisis and particularly in the 1930s, market liberalism endured as a critic of newer orthodoxies until it returned to dominance in the 1970s.

So firstly in this section, we consider the rise of organised labour as part of the rise of industrial capitalism, with the recognition and incorporation of trade unions not just as important organisations representing the voice of workers to employers and the state. We also examine the criticism of this compromise with labour, coming initially from the fringes of economic theory until it was drawn centrally into policy making with the rise of 'Thatcherism' and neoliberalism.

The Rise of Trade Unionism

From its beginning the relationship between labour and capital was far from clear-cut, with emergent capitalist employers seeking means to incorporate and control workers within the new systems of production. From the images passed down we see, on the one side, the 'dark satanic mills' and the grim workshops of Dickens where discipline was meted out with the big stick, or, on the other, the paternalistic regimes within the New Lanark mills of Robert Owen (see Box 1.3) or of Saltaire, the model mill town of Titus Salt. Since the new capitalists were often from the old feudal ruling class, or new aspirants who had taken on the trappings of a landed aristocracy, they attempted to preserve the deference of the past. From the 18th to the mid-19th century, when trade unions began to be formally recognised within law, the relations between employer and 'servants, labourers and work people' were governed by a series of

Masters and Servants Acts, where all the rights over control were vested with the 'master', while all potential penalties for breaching any conditions of employment – which included imprisonment – were the liability of the 'servant'.[3] Of course, there was no recourse for employees against bad employers, whatever the conditions they were required to endure.

Employment in the Industrial Revolution had its roots in established relations in agriculture and domestic workshops, the craft and cottage industries of pre-industrial Britain. Work would often be supplied through an intermediary system of contractors, the 'putting-out system.' This placed work within households, and responsibility for the organisation of work on familial authority, based around gender and age. Payment would be received for work completed, as a type of piecework system.[4] Rather than a move to direct employment, the move to large scale production did not involve individual and direct employment but internalised a subcontracting system rooted in domestic industry. Early factory, mill or mine owners had little or no immediate control over the workers or the nature of their work. Male skilled workers supervised

Box 1.3: *Robert Owen*

Initially an entrepreneur and manager in the textile industry, first at mills in Manchester and then at New Lanark in Scotland. Owen became renowned for improvement to the conditions for his employees, providing good housing, education, shorter working hours, and access to unsullied goods in the company shop. He later advocated the establishment of 'utopian' co-operative communities as the basis for a socialist society, ideas which led to the establishment of a number of such communities by Owen's followers. In 1832 Owen proposed the consolidation of trade unions which were growing rapidly, and independently, at the time. This resulted in the establishment of the Grand National Consolidated Trade Union which quickly established a membership of half a million. Owen led a protest of union members to petition the government against the sentence of the Tolpuddle Martyrs. The financial support for the many strikes in the period meant the union quickly went bankrupt, collapsing in 1834. Owen formulated his ideas in several books, including *A Report of the County of Lanark and A New View of Society*.

production and hired all auxiliary labour, sometimes their own wives and children, retaining familial authority and paying any wages from the money – based on output – agreed with the owner. Even within this arrangement, where payment was made for output, argument could ensue about quality and quantity of output. In mines, face-workers would contract for an area of the coal face and were paid for the coal cut, with other workers employed by the face-working team to transport the coal to the surface.[5] At the surface there could be argument with the owner's agent: how much coal should each gang of face workers be credited with? How much shale or other rock did it contain? Miners, way below ground and away from any argument, would appoint someone to negotiate for them.

The earliest attempt to regulate the labour market came with the *Ordinance of Labour* in the 14th century, where the crown attempted to halt a rise in wages when a third of the population were wiped out by the Black Death. Elizabethan England saw the beginnings of regulation concerning apprenticeship and entry into the skilled trades, as well as elementary health and safety. While not allowed to put pressure on employers to raise wages, which would have constituted a criminal conspiracy, representatives of these workers might bargain with employers collectively to establish a local 'rate for the job'. Prohibited from mobilising to put pressure on employers, early workers' organisation could attempt to ameliorate problems and insecurities through welfare benefits to members, for example providing benefits for unemployment, sickness, death, as well as acting as an employment agency for some trades. The only formal status of such embryonic trade unions was as friendly societies, a registered status they continued to have until the mid-20th century when a separate registration of trade unions was established.

Trade union organisation was initially restricted to the traditional crafts, to the 'aristocracy of labour', but by the early 19th century was spreading amongst the less skilled. These workers were sometimes more willing to take militant political and industrial action in defence of their interests and in support of their demands. Certainly, there was broad scope for protest, challenging the hours of work – the emergence of the 10-hour movement – security of employment, as well as concern with health and safety.

In the wake of the French Revolution, Parliament sought to contain any popular protest and introduced the *Combination Acts* of 1799 and 1800 (see Box 1.4) formally criminalising trade unions. Unions and their

Box 1.4: *Clause 3 – The Combination Act of 1800*

Every ... workman ... who shall at any time after the passing of this Act enter into any combination to obtain an advance of wages, or to lessen or alter the hours or duration of the time of working, or to decrease the quantity of work, or for any other purpose contrary to this Act, or who shall, by giving money, or by persuasion, solicitation or intimidation, or any other means, wilfully and maliciously endeavour to prevent any unhired or unemployed journeyman or workman, or other person, in any manufacture, trade or business, or any other person wanting employment in such manufacture, trade or business, from hiring himself to any manufacturer or tradesman, or person conducting any manufacture, trade or business, or who shall, for the purpose of obtaining an advance of wages, or for any other purpose contrary to the provisions of this Act, wilfully and maliciously decoy, persuade, solicit, intimidate, influence or prevail, or attempt or endeavour to prevail, on any journeyman or workman, or other person hired or employed, or to be hired or employed in any such manufacture, trade or business, to quit or leave his work, service or employment, or who shall wilfully and maliciously hinder or prevent any manufacturer or tradesman, or other person, from employing in his or her manufacture, trade or business, such journeymen, workmen and other persons as he or she shall think proper, or who, being hired or employed, shall, without any just or reasonable cause, refuse to work with any other journeyman or workman employed or hired to work therein, and who shall be lawfully convicted of any of the said offences, upon his own confession, or the oath or oaths of one or more credible witness or witnesses, before any two justices of the Peace for the county ... or place where such offence shall be committed, within 3 calendar months ... shall, by order of such justices, be committed to ... gaol for any time not exceeding 3 calendar months; or otherwise be committed to some House of Correction ... for any time not exceeding 2 calendar months.

From https://www.marxists.org/history/england/combination-laws/combination-laws-1800.htm

members faced a range of legal restrictions and had no protections for their funds. Attempts to influence wages or conditions at work could be interpreted as interfering with market forces, with 'restraint of trade.' Action by workers largely went underground, with organisation taking shape as the Luddite movement. Any actions or activities that trade unions might stage in support of their claims were illegal. State repression against any efforts at worker organisation could be violent. In August 1819, mounted militia sabre-charged a crowd of around 60,000 meeting in St Peters field on the outskirts of Manchester to demand Parliamentary reform, killing 15 and injuring perhaps 700 more. The experience of the Peterloo Massacre, and the cavalry charge, was to echo through to miners' experiences of picketing during their 1984 strike.

Trade unions continued in this precarious state. A Parliamentary Report of 1825 replicated the rules of many worker organisations, dealing mostly in welfare support for their members, but from funds which were far from secure.[6] In 1824 the prohibition on combination was repealed, making lawful attempts at influencing wages and conditions at work, as long as action was carried out 'peaceably and in a reasonable manner and without threat or intimidation to persuade others to cease or abstain from work.' Trade Unions themselves remained a legal anomaly, increasingly important but without any legal protection of their own funds.

Box 1.5: *The Chartists*

In 1838, following Parliament's failure to extend the franchise to working men in the 1832 Reform Act, members of the London Working Men's Association formulated six demands, 'the charter', which acted to mobilise working class action across the UK. The demands were for:
• Universal manhood suffrage
• Voting by secret ballot
• Constituencies of equal size
• Members of Parliament to be paid
• Abolition of the property qualification for becoming a Member of Parliament
• Annual Parliamentary elections
In the strike wave of the 1840s, mainly a response to pay cuts, the demands of the charter were often incorporated by workers.

Regularising Trade Unions?

Working class organisation, and militant action, were not restricted to trade unionism or demands restricted to improvements in pay and conditions at work. The fear of the ruling class was that these organisations also made demands with explicitly political ambitions. Chartism had been a voice of workers' protest with 'one man, one vote' achieved for the more affluent male householder in the 1867 *Reform Act* (see Box 1.5). The philosopher and Member of Parliament John Stuart Mill, in the absence of any female MPs, had unsuccessfully presented a petition to Parliament seeking an amendment to include women's suffrage on the same basis as men. The following year the Trade Union Congress (TUC) was established and pressure was building to achieve a working-class voice within Parliament. This established a separation of a 'political' sphere, for Parliamentary action, and an 'economic' sphere restricted precisely to pay and conditions at work, which was the legitimate territory for trade unions. Not only are the boundaries between the spheres often difficult, if not impossible, to determine but, by the late 19th century, there emerged a 'new unionism' organising the unskilled into general and industrial unions and often seeing their action in political terms. The separation of 'political' and 'economic' spheres was challenged by the emphasis on direct action by the syndicalism of new unionism. Strikes by these workers created concern in the media of the time, a concern which seems strikingly like newspaper accounts today. The writer in *Blackwood's Magazine* in 1867 presents the dispute as a challenge between the strikers and the wellbeing of innocent victims. The author argued that:

> 'a strike assumes a formidable aspect, and is by no means a subject of mirth, when the chief industry of a whole town or city is paralysed or destroyed by it; or when, as in the case of the cab and omnibus drivers of London - or, worse still, of the engine-drivers on any great line of railway converging to the capital - the affairs of the busiest community in the world are thrown into confusion, and the most serious hardship and wrong are inflicted upon thousands of innocent people.'[7]

The 1870s saw two important pieces of legislation which attempted to recognise, and regularise, the position of trade unions. In 1871 Parliament passed the first *Trade Union Act* which decriminalised trade union action 'in restraint of trade' (see Box 1.6). Instead, the Act established what became known as the 'golden formula', that trade union action – and the action of their officers – would have legal immunity if the action concerned was 'in pursuance of a trade dispute.' One problem with this formulation was that there was no clear definition of what constituted a trade dispute.

It was not only trade unions which had grown as distinct forms of organisation within the development of industrial capitalism. Early companies were involved in merchant adventurism; early trade and accumulation drawing from expansion of empire, including the trade in slaves. After several scandals – most notably the South Sea Bubble – which resulted from fraudulent activity by such companies, Parliament established limited liability for shareholders; the capacity for companies to 'incorporate', turning the commercial enterprise into an individual before the law. The corporation acquired a legal identity distinct from its shareholders or managers. It also meant the capacity to create 'multiple identities' in a web of wholly owned subsidiary corporations, each with their own independent activity and responsibilities.[8] Trade unions could not become corporate entities, so contracts they entered into were not legally enforceable. However, for the first time, with the passing of the 1871 Trade Union Act, their funds became protected through the establishment of trusts to hold their property, and the appointment of trustees to manage it.

The Act was a rather contentious concession to the trade unions and, at the same time, Parliament passed another which outlawed picketing. So, while taking trade union action out of criminal law, Parliament criminalised the unions' main weapon in any dispute. This was, however, short lived. Only four years later, in 1875, Parliament passed the *Conspiracy and Protection of Property Act*, which not only reversed the ban on picketing but also abolished the *Master and Servant Acts*, along with the *Employers and Workmen's Act*. The repeal of these two Acts decriminalised trade union action in terms of breach of the employment contract. While taken out of criminal law, unions were still open to civil law and claims

Box 1.6: *The Trade Union Act 1871, Section 2*

The purposes of any trade union shall not, by reason merely that they are in restraint of trade, be deemed to be unlawful so as to render any member of such trade union liable to criminal prosecution for conspiracy or otherwise.

of damage by employers or any other parties claiming harm from the impact of industrial action. According to Sidney and Beatrice Webb, these Acts were 'a fundamental revolution in law (see Box 1.7). Henceforth *master* and *servant* became *employer* and *employee*'.[9]

The work of the Webbs around the turn of the twentieth century indicates the coming of age of trade unions and collective bargaining.[10] They certainly presented a definition, and analysis, of trade unions which still shapes formal understanding (see Box 1.8). The assimilation of trade unions into Britain's political society that this definition might offer, as 'continuous associations', presents – or maybe legitimates – workers' organisation in terms of stable organisation in relationship with

---

Box 1.7: *Defining Trade Unions*

Sidney & Beatrice Webb, *History of Trade Unions* **(1920, original publication 1894)**

A Trade Union ... is a continuous association of wage earners for the purpose of maintaining or improving the conditions of their working lives.

Section 1 of the Trade Union and Labour Relations (Consolidation) Act 1992

In this Act a 'trade union' means an organisation (whether temporary or permanent) – (a) which consists wholly or mainly of workers of one or more descriptions and whose principal purposes include the regulation of relations between workers of that description or those descriptions and employers or employers' associations; or (b) which consists wholly or mainly of – (i) constituent or affiliated organisations which fulfil the conditions in paragraph (a) (or themselves consist wholly or mainly of constituent or affiliated organisations which fulfil those conditions), or (ii) representatives of such constituent or affiliated organisations, and whose principal purposes include the regulation of relations between workers and employers or between workers and employers' associations, or the regulation of relations between its constituent or affiliated organisations.

---

employers to find agreement on workers' terms and conditions. Ruled out were the occasional and often spontaneous strike committees which might form and, perhaps as quickly, disappear in discrete disputes. Also challenged is any notion of industrial democracy in terms of the establishment of workers' control. Within the Webbs' formulation trade unions are not seen as a challenge to existing economic order. The focus becomes a compromise between workers and management through collective bargaining, a democracy where – as later writers on workers' control would recognise[11] – rulers could not ultimately be replaced, and opposition would not become the governing party.

The Taff Vale Case and the Trade Disputes Act 1906

The regularising of the position of trade unions influenced the development of industrial militancy, with organisation and strikes amongst new groups of unskilled workers. The strike by women workers at the Bryant and May match factory was followed by the dockers in London and elsewhere. But it was rather the militancy of management, in their opposition to organised labour, which had the most important – if more hidden – impact on developments. In response to the increased organisation of labour, employers increasingly organised themselves, such as in the National Free Labour Association (NFLA), to recruit and supply scab labour to challenge union organisation and break strikes.

Perhaps the most significant dispute of the period occurred at the Taff

---

Box 1.8: *Sidney and Beatrice Webb*

The Webb's were members of the Fabian Society, which was one of the founding organisations of the Labour Party. Sidney was involved in writing the constitution for the new Labour Party and, in 1924, became an MP and Minister in its first government. Beatrice's background was in social research, having been involved in pioneering studies of poverty in London. Together they wrote many books on political and social issues, including *The History of Trade Unionism* and *Industrial Democracy,* which together established the foundation for the study of industrial relations in the UK and elsewhere. Together they were also involved in founding *The New Statesman* and the London School of Economics.

Vale Railway Company. The company had been established in 1836 to transport iron and coal from inland Wales to the port of Cardiff. In 1891 a profit scare and shareholder revolt led to the resignation of the company board. The company appointed a new manager, Ammon Beasley, who was renowned for opposition to trade unions. The railway workers were organised by the Amalgamated Society of Railway Servants (ASRS) but this was not recognised by the company. While there was no formal collective bargaining between the Taff Vale company and the ASRS, workers forwarded their complaints through delegations to the company management.

Following a strike by miners, the company withdrew its guarantee of a 60-hour week to the railway workers, meaning a cut in their wages. When signalmen sent a delegation to complain about the impact this had on their pay, one of the delegation was moved to another signal box a long way from his home. Rail workers saw this as victimisation by management, prompting their own strike action. The employers, in what was clearly a planned provocation, were prepared for such a response having already recruited outside labour to break a strike. Some of this scab labour came from retired railwaymen who had the skills needed to maintain the service, but most came from agencies such as the NFLA or from newspaper advertisements. Strike breakers were accommodated in dormitories arranged by the railway company. Leaflets, produced by the union and signed by its moderate general secretary, were distributed to the strike-breakers (see box 1.9). There was also rumour of sabotage by strikers to halt the trains driven by strike breakers, involving the cutting of signals and the greasing of track.

After 11 days of action the strikers returned to work. There hadn't been a resolution of the railway workers' concerns about pay and conditions, nor any promise of reinstatement for strikers or the victimised signalman. What the company promised was the establishment of a conciliation board to consider concerns. This was never established. Strike-breakers retained jobs at the railway, and many of the strikers were not given their jobs back. The day the strike ended, however, an injunction was served on two union officers who had put their name to what was claimed to be 'an improper circular' by referring to 'blacklegs' (see Box 1.9). The Taff Vale Railway Company also sued the union for damages resulting from the strike. Following the case, which ended in the House of Lords as the final court of appeal in 1901, the union was deemed liable and ordered to pay damages of £23,000 to the company, a sum which increased to £42,000 (or about £2.5 million

Box 1.9: *Union leaflet from Taff Vale Railway Strike, 1900*

STRIKE ON THE TAFF VALE RAILWAY

Mens Headquarters Cobourn Street Cathays

There has been a strike on the Taff Vale railway since Monday last. The management are using every means to decoy men here who they employ for the purpose of blacklegging the men on strike.

DRIVERS, FIREMEN, GUARDS, BRAKESMEN AND SIGNALMEN ARE ALL OUT.

Are you willing to be known as a BLACKLEG?

If you accept employment on the Taff Vale that is what you will be known by. On arriving at Cardiff, call at the above address where you can get information and assistance.

RICHARD BELL General Secretary.

(From Geoff Revell, *The Story of the Taff Vale Railway Strike* (National Union of Rail, Maritime and Transport Workers, 2008)

at today's equivalent) when costs were also added. The ruling was based on an 1898 case, of Joe Lyons and Sons v. Wilkins, where the court ruled that the use of the term 'blackleg' amounted to intimidation. Taff Vale, and other decisions by judges, made it impossible for trade unions to represent their members or take any action. Trade unions 'stood naked and unprotected at the altar of the common law.'[12]

The 1906 election proved a landslide victory for the Liberal Party, supported by 29 MPs from the Labour Representation Committee, who quickly established the Parliamentary Labour Party. Its priority was a reversal of the Taff Vale judgement, and the establishment of trade unions' place in civil society. The Labour Party, as the political voice of workers, needed the trade unions as an economic voice. This relationship required the marginalisation of other, more radical, alternatives which were fermenting: the syndicalism of the 'new' unions which increasingly

Box 1.10: *Trade Disputes Act 1906*

An act done in pursuance of an agreement or combination by two or more persons shall, if done in contemplation or furtherance of a trade dispute, not be actionable unless the act, if done without any such agreement or combination, would be actionable.

It shall be lawful for one or more persons, acting on their own behalf or on behalf of a trade union or of an individual employer or firm in contemplation or furtherance of a trade dispute, to attend at or near a house or place where a person resides or works or carries on business or happens to be, if they so attend merely for the purpose of peacefully persuading any person to work or abstain from working.

advocated direct action to radically transform society. This concession to labour was in the immediate wake of the 1905 revolution in Russia, which saw for the first time Soviets and Workers' Councils challenging the absolutist power of the Tsarist state.

In 1906 Parliament passed the *Trade Disputes Act* which gave immunity in civil law to trade unions and trade union officials for actions, including picketing, 'if done in contemplation or furtherance of a trade dispute' (see Box 1.10). It was important that any action would still be governed by a criminal law which might apply, for instance, in relation to any violence or intimidation. This point becomes central when considering the challenge to unions from neoliberalism.

This 1906 Act established the framework of law governing trade unions until the reforms of the *Industrial Relations Act* 1971 and, more substantially, until the law was transformed by the 'salami slicing' legislation of the Thatcher government. This legislation effectively reversed the 'voluntarism' of the post-1906 settlement and commenced the 'kettling' of the unions in the 1980s. The 1906 Act removed the offence of civil conspiracy, so making lawful acts by two or more people which would have been lawful for individuals. The right to peaceful picketing during a trade dispute was established, allowing strikers 'to attend at or near a house or place where a person resides or works or carries on business or for the purpose of peaceably obtaining or communicating information, or of peacefully persuading any person to work or abstain from working'.[13] It prevented injunctions against unions during a trade dispute for any breach of contract, thus preventing the sort of situation which had arisen in the Taff Vale case (see Box 1.11) What actually constituted a trade dispute was still left open.

One further judgement handed down by the House of Lords as a result of the Labour Party and its relationship to the trade unions (incidentally involving the same union as the Taff Vale case) still shapes contemporary debate. In December 1909, the Law Lords ruled that a trade union could

---

Box 1.11: *Contemporary Statutory Immunities*

3. It is a civil wrong, actionable in the civil courts, to persuade someone to break his contract of employment, or to secure the breaking of a commercial contract. But the law exempts from this liability those acting in contemplation or furtherance of a trade dispute, including - in certain circumstances - pickets themselves.

4. The exemption is provided by means of special "statutory immunities" to prevent liability arising to such civil law proceedings. These immunities ... have the effect that trade unions and individuals can, in certain circumstances, organise or conduct a picket without fear of being successfully sued in the courts. However, this protection applies only to acts of inducing breach, or interference with the performance, of contracts, or threatening to do either of these things.

5. These "statutory immunities" afford no protection for a picket, anyone involved in activities associated with picketing, or anyone organising a picket who commits some other kind of civil wrong – such as trespass or nuisance. Nor do they protect anyone – whether a picket, an employee who decides to take industrial action or to break his (sic) contract of employment because he is persuaded to do so by a picket, or anyone else - from the consequences which may follow if they choose to take industrial action or break their contracts of employment. These could include, for example, loss of wages, or other disciplinary action or dismissal from employment.

DBIS, *Code of Practice on Picketing* (London: Department for Business, Energy and Industrial Strategy, 2017), p. 2-3

---

not collect a levy from members which was to be used for political purposes, thus outlawing the financial support given by trade unions to the new Labour Party. Walter Osborne, a branch secretary of the ASRS and a Liberal Party supporter, had brought a case against the union, now with seriously depleted funds following the Taff Vale case, challenging the union levy supporting Labour. The decision was reversed in the Trade Union Act of 1915 which allowed union political funds, on condition that the union hold a ballot to establish one, and that it was kept separate from the general fund.

Voluntarism

The passing of the 1906 Act established the framework for labour relations until the 1970s. As the historian John Saville commented, 'for over half a century after the 1906 Act there were no fundamental changes in labour law or in the judicial decisions that were delivered in labour cases.'[14] Part of this apparent stability must rest with the weakness of trade unions in the period of economic recession and high unemployment, particularly after the General Strike of 1926 and the 1929 financial crash. The General Strike itself drew the only change in law, with the retribution of a move from contracting-out to contracting-in for member contributions to political funds legislated in the 1927 *Trade Disputes and Trade Unions Act*. This was later repealed in 1946 by the Labour Government.

The election of the Labour Government in 1945 brought the nationalisation of key sectors of the economy, such as steel, coal, and the railways. It also meant the establishment of the NHS and the welfare state. This new expanded state, as Davies and Freedland note, 'encouraged progressive employment practices presented as a model for all. This incorporated recognition of trade unions as the representative voice of workers, through a single channel of relations through collective bargaining at local and national levels. It also involved 'model' conditions of employment including paid holidays, sickness leave, and generous pension schemes.'[15] While certainly not establishing any form of industrial democracy – less any form of workers' control – which had been advocated by many pre-war socialists alongside nationalisation,[16] increasingly the trade unions were established as the representative voice of workers to employers and the State.

In other industrial countries the position of trade unions, their rights to representation, as well as right to strike, were becoming embedded in statutes. In the UK, regulation was largely left to the system of common law. Trade union recognition was left to voluntary agreement, and because neither trade unions nor employers' organisations were incorporated, any agreement reached was itself not enforceable in law. Because of this, the system of industrial relations that emerged in the UK was often referred to as 'voluntarism'. Otto Kahn-Freund, an influential legal theorist, called the system collective *laissez-faire* and famously argued in this respect that:

'There is, perhaps, no major country in the world in which the law has played a less significant role in the shaping of these relations than in Great Britain and in which today the law and the legal profession have less to do with labour relations.'[17]

The central feature, and apparent guarantor within industrial relations, was that the maintenance of industrial peace was through the establishment of collective bargaining.

'The desire of both sides of industry to provide for, and to operate, an effective system of collective bargaining is a stronger guarantee of industrial peace and of a smooth functioning of labour-management relations than any action legislators or courts or enforcement officers can ever hope to undertake.'[18]

Such an emphasis on collective bargaining characterised the work of the 'Oxford School' who strongly influenced industrial relations in the period, not least through their role on the Donovan Commission, the *Royal Commission on Trade Unions and Employers' Associations*, in the 1960s (see Section 2). However, while there was this belief in voluntary collective bargaining, generally promoted by the State, one measure to manage the economy was the use of pay policy. This was usually posed in terms of limits placed on pay rises, as 'guidance' to those involved in bargaining. The state itself – through the nationalised industries, welfare, and particularly the NHS – was the largest employer in the country and therefore a key actor in any such policy implementation.

A consequence of voluntarism is that in the UK there is no 'right to strike' or to organise. This has been 'a slogan ... such a right has not been bestowed by statute.'[19] What rights there are to withdraw labour or to entice others to do so, and hence to break their contract of employment, have tended to be drawn from international treaties and agreements. What explicit rights UK employees and trade unions have acquired has

Box 1.12: *European Social Charter*

Article 5 – The right to organise
With a view to ensuring or promoting the freedom of workers and employers to form local, national or international organisations for the protection of their economic and social interests and to join those organisations, the Parties undertake that national law shall not be such as to impair, nor shall it be so applied as to impair, this freedom. The extent to which the guarantees provided for in this article shall apply to the police shall be determined by national laws or regulations. The principle governing the application to the members of the armed forces of these guarantees and the extent to which they shall apply to persons in this category shall equally be determined by national laws or regulations.

Article 6 – The right to bargain collectively
With a view to ensuring the effective exercise of the right to bargain collectively, the Parties undertake:
1. to promote joint consultation between workers and employers;
2. to promote, where necessary and appropriate, machinery for voluntary negotiations between employers or employers' organisations and workers' organisations, with a view to the regulation of terms and conditions of employment by means of collective agreements;
3. to promote the establishment and use of appropriate machinery for conciliation and voluntary arbitration for the settlement of labour disputes; and recognise:
4. the right of workers and employers to collective action in cases of conflicts of interest, including the right to strike, subject to obligations that might arise out of collective agreements previously entered into.

European Council of Ministers, Turin, 18.X.1961

Available at: https://www.coe.int/en/web/conventions/full-list/-/conventions/rms/090000168006b642

been through international human rights conventions. The *European Social Charter*, Article 5, sets out the right to organise; Article 6 the right to strike (see Box 1.12). The Universal Declaration of Human Rights, while not explicitly mentioning trade union organisation or strikes, gives the right to peaceful assembly and association. While there was some challenge from the employers' representatives, recently the International Labour Organisation has reasserted the rights to organise and to withdraw labour. It might also be noted that the ILO has questioned the hiring of workers to replace strikers. They noted that:

'A special problem arises when legislation or practice allows enterprises to recruit workers to replace their own employees on legal strike. The difficulty is even more serious if, under legislative provisions or case-law, strikers do not, as of right, find their job waiting for them at the end of the dispute. The Committee considers that this type of provision or practice seriously impairs the right to strike and affects the free exercise of trade union rights.'[20]

The Enemy Within: the challenge to consensus

The industrial relations consensus, 'voluntarism', tended to be shared across the party-political divide. All parties seemed to recognise trade unions as the legitimate voice for workers, that employment terms and conditions should be resolved through voluntary agreement between unions and management, and that the law should not interfere beyond perhaps setting minimum conditions and standards. Law and the state should not interfere in the employment relationship other than in exceptional circumstances. Where trade unions had not been established their recruitment and recognition should be encouraged. This ethos tended to be followed by large private sector employers, and promoted within nationalised industries and the public sector more generally. Collective bargaining was the means of bringing the different sides of industry together and resolving differences. It was also a platform for establishing model employment rights including hours of work, paid holidays, pensions, as well as safety conditions within the workplace. When formal bargaining broke down then employers and trade unions might be brought together through some form of independent arbitration or conciliation with the possibility, in important cases, of the government stepping in to facilitate a compromise between parties.

For some on the political margins of the right, voluntarism gave far too much power and legitimacy to the trade unions, a critique which was ultimately to coalesce around Thatcherism and neoliberalism (see box 1.13). The basic assumption of this approach is one of individualism, an approach antithetical to those of trade unionism, almost by definition, based as it is on collectivism. Rather than collectivism, rooted in mutual support and assistance, neoliberalism bases itself on the assumption of competition between individuals in perpetual struggle for survival. The founding myth of liberal theories is usually some idea of a 'social contract' bringing together individuals to create political society from the original 'state of nature' of humanity. The exclusion of trade unions from legally binding contracts, therefore, is the exclusion of trade unions from society. Trade unions and collective bargaining are seen as an inherently violent threat to the very stability of the free society. As William Hutt puts it in *The Strike-Threat System*, a classic work of the neoliberal tradition:

> 'What actually goes under the name of 'collective bargaining' nearly always involves the strike threat ('the gun under the table'), in some countries even when the field is one in which strikes are illegal.'[21]

They are aware, of course, that other types of organisations – social clubs, as well as partnerships or co-operatives for instance – are unincorporated and unable to make legally binding contracts. But, in part, it is that trade unions are considered 'anti-market' by neoliberals that makes them different. '[Unions] alone, among the "voluntary" associations of this society,' Hutt argues, have:

> 'tended to use violent and coercive methods at every stage of their operations. No other species of private association has displayed as much corruption and arrogance as some trade unions have. No other private association has so habitually terrorized and exploited both members and non-members, or so institutionalized the practice of compelling persons to become members. The combination of poor performance and coercive practices is no mere coincidence. The poor performance of trade unions and their coercive practices are interacting causes and consequences.'[22]

While they rail at the immunity of trade unions, neoliberals make no mention of the rather surreal change to the capital entity or conglomerate when it is treated as an 'individual' by the process of incorporation. To the neoliberal, in terms of individuals making contracts on the free market, there is no qualitative difference – let alone difference in power – between the individual shopper or the multinational corporation.

Box 1.13: *Neoliberalism*

'Neoliberalism is in the first instance a theory of political economic practices that proposes that human well-being can best be advanced by liberating individual entrepreneurial freedoms and skills within an institutional framework characterized by strong private property rights, free markets, and free trade. The role of the state is to create and preserve an institutional framework appropriate to such practices. The state has to guarantee, for example, the quality and integrity of money. It must also set up those military, defence, police, and legal structures and functions required to secure private property rights and to guarantee, by force if need be, the proper functioning of markets. Furthermore, if markets do not exist (in areas such as land, water, education, health care, social security, or environmental pollution) then they must be created, by state action if necessary.'

David Harvey, *A Brief History of Neoliberalism* (London: Oxford University Press, 2007), p. 2

Neoliberalism is a school of economics which developed in the 1940s to challenge the growing dominance of Keynesianism and policies of state intervention. While arguing its roots lie in early market philosophy – drawing rather selectively on 18th century economists such as Adam Smith – this school largely developed in Austria in the 1920s as a critique of Marxism, socialism and all state involvement in the economy. Rather than the causes of the 1929 crash and 1930s recession being a failure of the 'free market', with the need for intervention, which was the prescription of the Roosevelt 'New Deal' policy and Keynesianism in the UK, neoliberals argued that it was state intervention itself which had caused the economic crisis.

These ideas were popularised by Hayek in 1944 who argued, in *The Road to Serfdom*, that any attempt at state intervention in the economy was the route to totalitarianism. While remaining fringe ideas throughout the 1950s and 1960s, attracting some support amongst academics and right-wing politicians, neoliberal ideas and policies were cultivated through meetings of the Mont Pelerin Society – founded by Frederich Hayek and involving important figures such as

George Stiglitz and Milton Friedman – as well as dissemination of their ideas through dedicated think tanks such as the Institute of Economic Affairs.
Forging a broad set of ideas on the nature of their market utopia, some formulated mechanisms and policies to move away from the interventionist state and economy. Neoliberal ideas became increasingly influential in the UK, and internationally, from the mid-1970s following the global crisis following the end of the Bretton Woods agreement which had governed international exchange. While the Callaghan government introduced some measure of 'monetarism' – the ideas associated with Milton Friedman to 'roll back the state' by cutting money available to the state – the move to neoliberalism as a guide and underpinning of policy is clearly most associated with Margaret Thatcher and governments after 1979. As the state withdraws from areas of activity, neoliberalism argues that the 'free market' and individual enterprise will successfully fill the gap.

Whilst arguing that the state should not intervene in or regulate the economy, leaving this to the 'free market', they see the state with the role of creating the conditions for, and defending, this 'free market'. So the 'free economy' goes along with a strong state required to defend the market against 'anti-market' behaviour and practice. This is therefore totally consistent with defence of repressive 'law and order' regimes, it also is antagonistic to trade union organisation which neoliberalism claims to be 'anti-market' in the use of 'monopoly practices' such as the closed shop and picketing during industrial action.

Therefore, there is no difference between the purchaser or seller of labour power, with each addressing and contracting each other as equal individuals.

Until the mid-1970s these views were largely marginal, with any intellectual expression coming through small fringe organisations: the Mont Pelerin Society (MPS) established in Switzerland in 1947 as an intellectual gathering of neoliberal thinkers, as well as the Institute of Economic Affairs (IEA) established in London in 1956 to promote these ideas in the UK. Neoliberalism has been associated most prominently

50

with Fredrich von Hayek, particularly through his 1944 book *The Road to Serfdom.*[23] At the very point at which the post-war Labour government established the NHS and welfare state, as well as adopt Keynesian methods to attempt management of the periodic crises of the economy, Hayek argued that any state intervention would bring tyranny and totalitarianism. Hayek was particularly opposed to the 1906 *Trade Disputes Act*, which he saw as a spectacular 'privilege by the unions' which put them above the law.[24]

An important starting point for understanding the neoliberal approach to trade unions is through the work of Sylvester Petro, a Professor of Law at New York University. Petro prepared various papers on trade unions and industrial relations for early meetings of the Mont Pelerin Society and was a major influence on Hayek's thinking.[25] He also set the agenda for a shift in policy prescription away from voluntarism, the collectivist consensus, towards a 'free market' approach. In common with other neoliberals Petro argues that the basis of 'the free society', a phrase used as synonymous with capitalism, is private property and freedom of contract: 'personal freedom cannot even be conceived outside the environment provided by property and contract rights.'[26] Petro claimed that trade unions had never been illegal, arguing that they always benefited from special privilege. He also denied that the 'free market' led to exploitation or inequality. Rights of private property were equal, and the impact of trade unions and collective bargaining were to see the employment of violence to move part of the wage pool from the unorganised to the organised.

> 'Many are concerned today over the plight of the nation's teachers, whose incomes have not kept pace while the prices of the things they buy have been soaring. Many other members of society – pensioners and those not in a position to exert monopolistic pressures – suffer in exactly the same way. They ought to know the real cause of their disagreeable position. Unions and their members can and do raise their own wages over free-market levels; but in each and every instance that they do, they exploit their fellow workers and consumers. Compulsion and coercion as normal union methods, therefore, do not exhaust their vicious effects in the corruption and mismanagement of unions alone. They have untoward consequences for all workers and for society as a whole.'[27]

There is no consideration of the overall share going to wages as, according to Petro, this is fixed by the market with low wages or incomes being the fault of organised workers, through monopoly trade unions,

51

able to grab more than their share.

Little consideration is given to what determines the size of this wage pool, somehow it emerges as the outcome of the market. Low pay is thus presented as the fault of trade unions exerting their 'monopoly': monopoly power which comes from closed shop contracts and the 'one out all out' strategy of unions in industrial action.

The cause of militancy in unions, Petro claims, is usually because politically motivated or just inept officers mislead an essentially moderate and reasonable membership. This does not mean that Petro is against the right to strike, 'a fundamental right of working men in a free society.'[28] This also entails, for him, rights for employers, 'where workers were dissatisfied with their wages, they had a common-law right to cease work in concert. But they violated the law if they used force or fraud to prevent other workers from seeking the jobs they vacated. For such forcible prevention negated the right of employers to seek other workers, and the right of other workers to seek employment.'[29] This, therefore, involves making not strikes but picketing an illegal act since: '[t]o permit a union to block the access of a struck employer to these free-market alternatives is to give that union the privilege of destroying the free market - the privilege, in short, of expropriating the struck employer, the striker replacements, and the outside businessmen who are strangers to the [labour] dispute.'[30] The nature of a free society means, therefore, that the employer also has the right to 'discourage membership' of trade unions and to dismiss strikers, 'while the law should, precluding the occasion and the context of intimidation, confine organized workers to the basic right to strike. To permit strikers to congregate at the scene of the labor dispute is to invite violence.'[31]

Petro does see a role for trade unions in the USA and other societies, devoid of their capacity to withdraw labour. One is as individual representation, perhaps against 'the stupid, ignorant, unfair, forman ... one of the real problems of a free society.'[32] More important, and remembering he is writing largely about the USA in the 1950s, they could serve as a central part of social welfare:

'There are any number of other ways in which unions can serve both their members and society as a whole. They could provide employees with a great many useful services. They could be of great help to their members in planning savings and investment programs. If they were run well, they could be trusted with pension and welfare plans. They can and do run training and retraining schools for workers who are anxious to improve their productivity.

They could serve as a clearing-house as regards employment opportunities. They could, in short, do many things that they are not doing at all now, or doing only rudimentarily and half-heartedly.'[33]

A further feature of Petro's argument is also worth noting here. He argues that history has taken the wrong course, that:

'[in] many ways we may have gone backward. We do not see some things as clearly today as they were seen by the best men of politics and law in the eighteenth century. I do not think that we would be setting back the clock if we were to create the juridical structure which they planned and set forth in the Constitution. On the contrary, such an operation would in my opinion require us to adjust the clock, and our minds, forward.'[34]

The central purpose of Petro's book is to propose means by which the USA could scrap much of the industrial relations regulation, allowing for a move towards his free market utopia based around individual property rights. This involves scrapping many of the trade union and employment rights established in the USA in the 1930s and 1940s, breaking the 'monopoly power' of trade unions and abolishing the right to picket:

'the effect of the [labour] relations legislation was to extinguish another right recognized by the common law: the right of employers to resist and discourage employee organization by means of the peaceful exercise of their own property and contract rights.'[35]

The Establishment of Trade Unionism and its Growing Challenge

Embedded within Petro are the arguments around picketing, and workers' rights which reach a crescendo in the 1970s and 1980s. They re-emerge at the peak of strike action, and produce the rationale for Conservative legislation containing the actions of trade unions. We find in Petro several themes which reappear in neoliberal argument on trade unions. Firstly, the claim that the unions exert monopoly power through closed shop agreements. Second, that trade union officers with political motives take advantage of a more gullible, and moderate, membership willing to accept the legitimate offer on terms and conditions at work offered by employers. Third, that trade unions have benefited from some special treatment that puts them above the law, particularly when taking industrial action.

Because of the conservativism of the UK legal system, rather averse to any change, the trade unions were accommodated through the granting of immunities for limited activities when associated with a trade dispute. Until the 1980s, as we shall see in the next section, there was no piece of legislation which both established the position of trade unions and governed their activities and management. While 'voluntarism', built around free collective bargaining between employers and trade unions, held for more than half a century there was not unanimity on the settlement. There remained a challenge from a fringe of politicians and academics who rejected not just the dominant economic management but also the compromise with labour. This view was to move to the centre ground in the economic crisis of the 1970s.

The central cause of Britain's economic problems was presented as the 'special privileges' of the 1906 *Trade Disputes Act*. Hayek himself frequently railed against the Act. In 1977 he wrote to *The Times* arguing that 'there is no salvation for Britain until the special privileges granted to the trade unions by the *Trade Disputes Act of 1906* are revoked … the privileges then granted to the trade unions have become the chief source of Britain's economic decline.'[36] He, like Petro, argues that it is trade union monopoly power which is the cause of industrial conflict,

> 'in many countries voluntary associations of workers had only just become legal when they began to use coercion to force unwilling workers into membership and to keep non-members out of employment. Most people probably still believe that a 'labo[u]r dispute' normally means a disagreement about remuneration and the conditions of employment, while as often as not its sole cause is an attempt on the part of the unions to force unwilling workers to join.'[37]

An attack on the Act was also staged by Hayek's disciples. Keith Joseph, a key figure in the 'neoliberal turn' and soon to enter the Thatcher government, argued in 1979 that: 'our unions have been uniquely privileged for several decades … In a trade dispute, most things seem permitted for the union side; breaking contracts; inducing others to break contracts; picketing of non-involved companies; secondary boycotts.'[38] Disputes are promoted by a union leadership which sees free enterprise as class enemy, that 'taught workers to resist efficiency, obstruct management, insist on over-manning, resent profit and ignore consumers.'[39]

The project for neoliberals, as we shall see in the next section, was to reverse the position of the trade unions established by 1906. The

Thatcher government, drawing on the work of Hayek and other neoliberals, set about the 'kettling' of the trade unions, the transformation of employment, along with attempting to establish their utopia of the free market economy.

Notes

1. Eric Hobsbawm, *Labouring Men: Studies in the History of Labour* (London: Weidenfeld & Nicolson, 1964)
2. Carter L. Goodrich, *The Frontier of Control: A Study in British Workshop Politics* (London: Pluto Press, 1975, original publication 1921)
3. E.P. Thompson found the continuance of this call for deference well into the 1970s, continuing in the letters columns of the newspapers especially where there is a withdrawal of labour reflecting the persistence of concern of 'the servant problem'. E. P. Thompson, "Sir, Writing by Candlelight," in *Writing by Candlelight* (London: Merlin, 1980), p.39-48
4. See for example the discussion in Stephen A. Marglin, "What Do Bosses Do? the Origins and Functions of Hierarchy in Capitalist Production," *Review of Radical Political Economics* 6, no. 2 (1974) and William Lazonick, Business Organization and the *Myth of the Market Economy* (Cambridge University Press, 1993)
5. In some mining areas in the UK this was referred to as the 'butty' system. A similar system of contracting in mining in France is given by Emile Zola in his 1885 novel *Germinal*
6. https://www.marxists.org/history/england/combination-laws/1825/combinations.pdf
7. Blackwood's Magazine, "Strikes and Trades' Unions, 1867," in *Trade Unions in the Victorian Age,* Debates on the issue from 19th century critical journals, Volume IV 1865-1870 (Farnborough: Gregg International, 1973), p. 719-20
8. For an interesting and brief account, see Daniel Bennett, *A Brief History of Corporations: Where Did They Come From?* (Bristol Radical Pamphleteer, Pamphlet 3, 2009)
9. History of Trade Unions, cited by Otto Kahn-Freund, "Legal Framework," in *The System of Industrial Relations in Great Britain,* ed. H. A. Clegg and Allan Flanders (Oxford: Basil Blackwell, 1956), p.42-127, fn. 2 p. 46
10. Sidney Webb and Beatrice Webb, *The History of Trade Unionism,* originally published 1894 and *Industrial Democracy,* 1897

11. Ken Coates and Tony Topham, *The New Unionism: The Case for Workers' Control* (Harmondsworth: Penguin Books, 1972)

12. Hugh Collins, K.D. Ewing, and Aileen McColgan, *Labour Law* (Cambridge: Cambridge University Press, 2012), p. 665

13. Cited in James G. Moher, "Trade Unions and the Law – History and a Way Forward?" *History & Policy*, 2007; available from http://www.historyandpolicy.org/policy-papers/papers/trade-unions-and-the-law-history-and-a-way-forward

14. John Saville, "The Trade Disputes Act of 1906,"*Historical Studies in Industrial Relations* Vol. 1 (1996), p. 39

15. Paul Davies and Mark Freedland, *Labour Legislation and Public Policy*, Clarendon Law Series (Oxford: Oxford University Press, 1993), p. 9

16. For a sample of these writings see Ken Coates and Tony Topham, *Workers' Control: A Book of Readings and Witnesses for Workers' Control* (Panther, 1970)

17. Otto Kahn-Freund, "Legal Framework," in *The System of Industrial Relations in Great Britain*, ed. H. A. Clegg and Allan Flanders (Oxford: Basil Blackwell, 1956), p. 43

18. Ibid, p. 43

19. Maurice Kay LJ, cited in Hugh Collins, K.D. Ewing, and Aileen McColgan, *Labour Law* (Cambridge: Cambridge University Press, 2012), p. 663

20. *Record of Proceedings. International Labour Conference*, Geneva, 81st Session, para. 175, 1994, cited in Bernard Gernigon, Alberto Odero, and Horacio Guido, *ILO Principles Concerning the Right to Strike* (Geneva: International Labour Organization, 1998)

21. William H. Hutt, *The Strike-Threat System: The Economic Consequences of Collective Bargaining* (New York: Arlington House, 1973) p. 43

22. Sylvester Petro, *The Labor Policy of the Free Society* (New York: Ronald Press, 1957), p. 109

23. F.A. Hayek, *The Road to Serfdom* (London: George Routledge & Sons Ltd, 1944).

24. See e.g. F.A. Hayek, *A Tiger by the Tail* (London: Institute of Economic Affairs, 1972), p. 67

25. See Yves Steiner, "The Neoliberals Confront the Trade Unions," in *The Road from Mont Pelerin: The Making of the Neoliberal Thought Collective*, ed. Philip Mirowski and Dieter Plehwe (Harvard University Press Cambridge, MA, 2009), p.181-203.

26. Ibid, p. 37

27. Sylvester Petro, p. 116-7

28. Ibid, p. 113
29. Ibid, p. 193
30. Ibid, p. 252
31. Ibid, p. 196
32. Ibid, p. 107
33. Ibid, p. 108
34. Ibid, p. 289
35. Ibid, p. 138
36. F.A. Hayek, Trade Unions: "Trade Union Immunity Under the Law" (Hayek Letter) [Revoke Privileges Granted By Trade Disputes Act, 1906] (1977); available from http://www.margaretthatcher.org/document/114630
37. F.A. Hayek, *A Tiger By the Tail* (London: Institute of Economic Affairs, 1972), p. 67
38. Keith Joseph, *Solving the Union Problem Is the Key to Britain's Recovery* (London: Centre for Policy Studies, 1979)
39. Ibid, p. 6

Chapter 2
Containing the Unions

The Attack on Voluntarism

By the mid-20th century, after more than fifty years of voluntarism, there was an increasing argument to contain trade unions. Firstly, there was recognition of the UK's relative economic decline against industrial competitor nations, particularly Germany and Japan which appeared to have more formal and collaborative labour relations. Second, post-war full employment had strengthened trade unions, particularly in the workplace. There developed what some commentators called 'the British disease': incidences of short, unofficial, and spontaneous – 'wild-cat' – strike action, particularly within some industries such as motor manufacture. Concerns mounted over not just the increasing number of strikes, but that around 95% of these were unofficial, outside of established agreements and disputes procedures and therefore the formal control of the trade unions. Such actions were usually organised by workplace representatives – shop stewards – who became a 'folk devil' of 1950s and 1960s British society with the image, cultivated in popular cinema and TV, that they posed a continual threat of walkouts.[1] Rather than point to other causes of the UK's economic malaise – a failure of investment, poor management, a lack of training, a contempt for trade or manufacturing – to which the industrial relations pattern was likely itself a symptom, the blame was increasingly being put on organised labour.

Harold Wilson's Labour Government, elected in 1964, established a *Royal Commission on Trade Unions and Employers Associations,* known as the *Donovan Commission,* which argued for voluntarism with the extension of formal collective bargaining into the workplace. According to research for the *Commission* shop stewards were the 'lubricant' to good relations between employer and employee, rather than troublemakers prompting walk-outs at every opportunity. While, ideologically, there may have been support from the Labour government for free collective bargaining between unions and management, as a means of reaching agreements on pay and conditions, collective bargaining was under pressure from the economic cycle. Increasingly, the government fell back on prices and income policies, putting limits on potential pay rises when rising inflation was becoming the central economic concern.

In part because of some high-profile strikes, the government drew up

> **Box 2.1:** *In Place of Strife: Labour Government proposals for industrial relations reform in 1968*
>
>
> • Registration of collective agreements, and to make some agreements legally binding if provision for this is expressly included in the agreement.
> • Rights of trade unions to receive company information, subject to commercial sensitivities.
> • New rules on Friendly societies, the creation of a new Registrar of Trade Unions and Employers' Associations, a post to be combined initially with that of the Registrar of Friendly Societies.
> • Commission on Industrial Relations with powers to arrange ballots for union recognition and audit union finances.
> • Power of the Secretary of State to enforce 28-day cooling-off period against strikes or lock-outs if unconstitutional or if inadequate negotiation had taken place. Secretary of State to be able to call for strike ballot when action considered "a serious threat to the economy."
> • Create a new Registrar of Trade Unions and Employers' Associations, a post to be combined initially with that of Registrar of Friendly Societies
>
> DBIS, *Code of Practice on Picketing* (London: Department for Business, Energy and Industrial Strategy, 2017), p. 2-3

proposals for the restriction and limitation of trade union action. Merchant sailors struck in 1966 which the Prime Minister, Harold Wilson, described as the work of politically motivated men.[2] Instead of following the Donovan recommendations, the government proposed its own measures to contain industrial action and the unions. Barbara Castle, Secretary of State for Employment, put forward the White Paper, *In Place of Strife*, which argued the need for 'limiting the number of serious unconstitutional strikes and inter-union disputes' (see Box 2.1). She proposed the mandatory registration of unions and collective agreements. Most contentiously, she proposed that the Secretary of State might, if they considered there had been inadequate negotiation, have the power to impose a 28-day cooling-off period in disputes. The

Minister should also be given the power to call for a ballot before industrial action. Support for collective bargaining was given in the White Paper, with a proposal for greater transparency of company information and allowing access to trade unions.

The measures were opposed by the unions and some members of the Labour cabinet. After discussions between Wilson and Castle with the TUC General Council, the proposals were withdrawn. They came to an agreement that the TUC would examine 'measures for limiting the number of serious unconstitutional strikes.'[3]

Heath, the 'Quiet Revolution' and the Industrial Relations Act

Heath's Conservative government was elected in 1970 in an atmosphere of growing economic crisis and challenges to the economic consensus of the post-war years. During their period in opposition the Conservative Party had begun to explore free market economics as an alternative to Keynesian interventionism. In government they launched a 'quiet revolution' shifting from economic and industrial policy to reliance on market forces, where failing and inefficient companies would be allowed to fail.[4] This 'lame ducks' policy was to quickly become a problem, particularly with the collapse of Rolls Royce, leading to a U-turn in economic policy. Industrial relations policy also proved a failure for the Heath government.

During the opposition period a group of Conservative barristers, including Geoffrey Howe who was to become Chancellor of the Exchequer in the Thatcher government, picked up on a key point in Hayek's argument. The group proposed that trade unions should forfeit their immunities – which they present as privileges – unless they register as friendly societies and thus lose control over their own rule books. While insisting that state involvement within the economy be minimised, they argued for greater controls over trade unions: the development of a 'free economy and strong state.'[5] The Conservative Party produced their own proposals in a paper, *Fair Deal at Work*,[6] which set out a comprehensive reshaping of voluntarism by the introduction of a legislative framework in an *Industrial Relations Bill*. By giving the unions corporate status, the issue of 'immunities' would be cleared, making them liable for compensation and damages for breach of contract in what might be defined as unlawful industrial action. This could be avoided, suggested the proposal, by the formal registration of unions. It proposed that collective bargaining contracts should be legally binding, unless the parties to the contract explicitly opt out. The closed shop, while not looked upon favourably, would be tolerated only if it was established following a ballot of the workforce. The white paper further proposed a separate National Industrial Relations Court (NIRC), as a specialist branch of the High Court, to deal with any issues referred to it concerning individual and collective disputes, appeals concerning registration, arbitration, and granting injunctions during industrial disputes. Central to this was the creation of 'unfair industrial practices', a range of relatively unspecified activities, carried out by employers, workers, or unions: these could include infringement of right to join, or not join, a trade union; unfair dismissal; or breaking a ruling of the NIRC.[7]

It was claimed that the *Industrial Relations Act* was 'promoting good industrial relations ... of collective bargaining freely conducted on behalf of workers and employers and with due regard to the interests of the community' (see Box 2.2). Further, the Act supported the principle

'of developing and maintaining orderly procedures in industry for the peaceful and expeditious settlement of disputes by negotiation, conciliation or arbitration, ... of free association of workers in independent trade unions, and of employers in employers' associations, so organised as to be representative, responsible and effective bodies for regular relations between employers and workers; and ... freedom and security for workers, protected by adequate safeguards against unfair industrial practices, whether on the part of employers or others.'[8]

While this might have seemed in accord with the general aspirations of trade unions it required their registration, and hence loss of control over rule books, which was soundly rejected by the TUC and most unions. Further controls were seen in the Industrial Relations Court and other institutions established by the Act. In March, an unofficial strike against the Bill was supported by about 1.5 million trade union members, although not formally by the TUC.

Industrial action was generally on the increase, and getting more militant. In early 1972 the NUM staged its first national strike since 1926. Following a withdrawal of government funding Upper Clyde Shipbuilders went into receivership, and the shop stewards' committee retaliated by staging a work-in at the yards. Increasingly the Heath governments policy seemed to be breaking the foundation of Britain's

Box 2.2: *The Industrial Relations Act 1971*

• Establishment of an Industrial Relations Court, a Registrar of Trade Unions, along with formal role for the Commission on Industrial Relations to deal with ballots.
• Workers given the right to join, or not to join, a trade union.
• Collective agreements to be assumed to be legally enforceable unless a formal disclaimer included in its terms.
• Closed shop allowed, with workers given an option of alternative payment to charity.
• Registration of trade unions and employers' associations, with only registered unions gaining immunities in trade disputes and other benefits of the Act.
• Employee rights against unfair dismissal.
• Rules on trade union recognition.
• Powers of the Secretary of State, through the IRC, to call for cooling-off period and ballot to halt industrial action in some circumstances.
• Limitations on rights of picket.

industrial economy, and unemployment increased to an unprecedented post-war level of over one million. Following the breakdown of national bargaining in the engineering industry around fifty occupations took place following threats of lock-outs. Workplace occupations became a significant tactic against closures and lock-outs.[9] Most important for the fate of the *Industrial Relations Act,* dock workers staged a national campaign against the introduction of standardised containers – containerisation – in cargo handling. Following transport companies taking their case against dock workers refusing to handle their lorries to the Industrial Relations Court, five London dockers were imprisoned for contempt after refusing to recognise the court as part of the campaign against the Act which set it up.

The Act was not the only issue causing industrial tensions. More significant was the government's attempted move towards wage restraint intended to tackle rising unemployment. In 1971 the government introduced a wage freeze, followed by limits of £1+4% and, in a final stage, 7% or £2.85 per week dependent on which was highest. These limits did not match the increasing levels of inflation which hit 15% in the early 1970s

Box 2.3: *Employment and Trade Union Related Legislation: Labour Government 1974-9*

Trade Union and Labour Relations Act 1974
* Repeal of the Industrial Relations Act
* Employment Protection Act 1975 (and Consolidation Act 1978)
* Establishment of Acas (Advisory, Conciliation and Arbitration Service)
* Established a trade union recognition procedure
* Duty of employers to disclose information
* Individual employment rights including maternity and unfair dismissal
* Right to time off for trade union duties
* Rights on dismissal and redundancy
* Right to a written statement of pay and deductions
* Written contract of employment with any changes requiring agreement of employee

Trade Union and Labour Relations (Amendment) Act 1976
* Widened union immunity from civil action

Also:

Health and Safety at Work Act 1974
* Established Health & Safety Executive
* Trade union workplace health & safety representatives

Sex Discrimination Act 1975
* Established the Equal Opportunities Commission
* Outlawed gender discrimination in recruitment and employment

Race Relations Act 1976
* Established Race Relations Commission.
* Prohibited discrimination on racial grounds in the areas of employment, education, and the provision of goods, facilities and services and premises

and peaked at around 25% by the middle of the decade. Workers were told to 'tighten their belts'. In their first national strike since 1926 the NUM demanded a substantial increase and, as 'a special case', a Commission under Lord Wilberforce awarded them an increase of 21 per cent.[10]

Another issue was to have long term and profound implications, not just for industrial relations. The Heath government negotiated terms for UK entry into what was then the European Economic Community (EEC) which consisted of nine countries at the time. The Labour opposition, following pressure from Tony Benn and the left of the party, promised a referendum on entry if they won the election in 1974. These exact political positions were to shift in the following decade with the EEC moving to become the European Union, which, while maintaining the free market, instituted some level of employee protection just as this was being rolled back in the UK.

Labour and the Social Contract

With the significant level of campaigning against it, particularly the refusal of trade unions to register, the *Industrial Relations Act* had become unworkable – and effectively defunct – within two years. The Act was finally repealed by the incoming Labour Government in 1974 through the *Trade Union and Labour Relations Act 1974* (see Box 2.3). Labour had first been elected as a minority government following Heath going to the country over a fuel crisis which was itself brought on by an oil crisis and a second strike by miners. Initially, with a seemingly radical program, the new government not only scrapped the *Industrial Relations Act,* largely returning to the prior situation of voluntarism, they claimed a concordat – the Social Contract – with the unions to bring harmony to industrial relations. In exchange for industrial peace with union acceptance of a pay policy, the government promised a range of employment and social legislation (see Box 2.3). Initially, the Social Contract with the unions meant the introduction of a range of legislation attempting to improve industrial relations through support for collective bargaining as well as individual job rights. This did not last and, contentiously, the emphasis moved towards pay restraint as the economy remained in crisis. Tensions increased as inflation quickly eroded living standards and limits on pay undermined collective bargaining and the relationship between trade unions, government and the state.

The central piece of industrial relations reform introduced by the Labour government was the *Employment Protection Act 1975.* This established a range of industrial relations agencies which remain important more than three decades later. First it established the Advisory, Conciliation and Arbitration Service (Acas) which was 'charged with the general duty of promoting the improvement of industrial relations, and in particular of encouraging the extension of collective bargaining and, where necessary, reform of collective bargaining machinery.' This went along with the establishment of two other bodies, the Central Arbitration Council and, to replace the role of the Registrar of Friendly Societies in this area, the Certification Officer for Trade Unions and Employers' Associations.

To facilitate collective bargaining, procedures were established for Acas to supervise a recognition procedure. This procedure allowed for a ballot of employees at a workplace to establish support for trade union representation. Where collective bargaining was established, the Act gave employee representatives, who they asumed would be male, rights to information. As the Act put it, 'it shall be the duty of the employer ...',

'to disclose to those representatives on request all such information relating to his undertaking as is in his possession, or that of any associated employer, and is both -
(a) information without which the trade union representatives would be to a material extent impeded in carrying on with him such collective bargaining, and
(b) information which it would be in accordance with good industrial relations practice that he should disclose to them for the purposes of collective bargaining.'[11]

To support collective bargaining further, the Act made provision for employee representatives to be given both training for their role and time to perform their trade union duties.

'An employer shall permit an employee of his who is an official of an independent trade union recognised by him to take time off, subject to and in accordance with subsection (2) below, during the employee's working hours for the purpose of enabling him -
(a) to carry out those duties of his as such an official which are concerned with industrial relations between his employer and any associated employer, and their employees; or
(b) to undergo training in aspects of industrial relations which is -
(i) relevant to the carrying out of those duties;

and
(ii) approved by the Trades Union Congress or by the independent trade union of which he is an official.'[12]

Not only did this lead to agreements to allow training and the provision of time to act as representatives, but also for facilities such as office space, use of telephones, and other necessary provisions to carry out the role of an employee representative.

As well as support for collective bargaining the Act sought to address some of the key issues facing workers. Most pressing, in the mid-1970s, was the issue of closures and redundancy. Since the late 1960s, workers had been faced with growing unemployment due to factory closures and redundancies and, initially, this had been seen by policy makers as a problem of mobility. Unemployed workers should have some encouragement or assistance to move from areas with declining industries to find available work. The proposed solution was the *Redundancy Payments Act 1965*. Instead of resolving these supposed imbalances in employment, the original intention of the Act, the payments were being used to buy workers out of jobs, deployed within collective bargaining to come to a compromise over redundancy and closures.

Simultaneous with the passing of the *Employment Protection Act*, the Secretary of State for Industry in the Labour Government, Tony Benn, who had been a very public supporter of the UCS work-in, was in the process of giving financial backing to three workers' cooperatives which had arisen after workers challenged closure plans. One impact of the *Employment Protection Act* might have been that it stifled such militant responses to closure, extending the consultation to 90-days when over 100 or more workers were involved in redundancy.

Rights were extended for sickness and maternity leave. Rights and protections were also enhanced in other pieces of legislation, which would have a significant impact on trade unions: sex and race discrimination legislation included elements which impacted directly on job recruitment and treatment in employment.

The passing of the *Health and Safety at Work Act* granted legal recognition and a specific role for employee representatives with the creation of the health and safety representative (see Box 2.3). This Act was possibly a redeemer of the workplace trade union representative, becoming the model for new roles for equality and learning representatives that developed in the more insecure years that were to come.

An attempt to move towards some form of industrial democracy, with worker representatives having places on company boards, amounted to nothing following the failure of the Bullock Commission. In August 1975, shortly after the referendum ratifying UK membership of the EEC, or 'Common Market', the government established a Commission of Inquiry under Lord Bullock to examine corporate governance. The terms of reference for the inquiry accepted:

> 'the need for a radical extension of industrial democracy in the control of companies by means of representation on boards of directors, and accepting the essential role of trade union organisations in this process, to consider how such an extension can be achieved ... Having regard to the interests of the national economy, employees, investors and consumers, to analyse the implications of such representation for the efficient management of companies and for company law.'[13]

The inquiry was to investigate employee involvement mechanisms in Europe, such as the role of supervisory boards in Germany where there was equal representation from workers and shareholders, as well as proposals from the TUC and other interested parties. The inquiry opened a number of contentious issues, not least around 'management's right to manage'. Importantly it also concerned the role of trade unions in employee representation. While in Germany the system of 'codetermination' was based on employee representation through a system of works councils, UK trade unions had been insistent on a single channel of representation around trade unions and collective bargaining. The TUC were insistent that any extension of industrial democracy must be as an extension of collective bargaining. This proved an anathema for employer representatives on the Commission of Inquiry. Pointing to fragmented trade union structures and workplaces where there was limited or no union membership, they argued, in their minority report, that:

> 'Industrial democracy' is a term which can all too easily be applied to a wide range of developments, some good, some, in our view, bad ... the appointment of 'worker directors' – by which we understand people from the shop floor elected or appointed directly on to Boards of Directors as we know them now – would not be helpful. Certainly it is unwise to impose 'democracy' on those who are unwilling or unready to receive it.[14]

With this attitude from employers, which echoed the post-colonial mind set of Britain's elites, and with trade unions reluctant to open broader channels of representation, the Bullock Commission's main proposal was quickly forgotten. The proposal was to establish company boards with equal shareholder and employee representation alongside independent members, the '2X + Y' board composition. More than a quarter of a century later, with the trade unions seriously weaker, and as the EU passed its Directives on the consultation of employees (see below), the UK proved the only member state at the time where no formal mechanisms existed to consult employees on major corporate decisions such as redundancies.

The period after the mid-1970s saw a growing assault on workers and trade unions. Weaknesses in the recognition procedure became apparent with a long running dispute at Grunwick. When workers at the photo processing plant walked out because of working conditions, they failed to get recognition for the union they had joined because their employer refused any cooperation with Acas or the recognition procedure. The dispute, instead, became a *cause célèbre* around mass picketing which was established to support the striking workers.

The fate of the Social Contract is generally well known. In the context of a fiscal crisis, the UK government, with some prompting from the International Monetary Fund, instituted public sector cuts along with pay restraint. After three years of 'voluntary' wage restraint, alongside continuing inflation, living standards were continuing to slide. With the prospect of another year where pay rises were restricted to 5% and with inflation at around twice this amount, the hold on trade unions broke with a push to break the limit on pay. Strikes occurred as workers challenged the limits, first in the private sector. For example, at Ford where, after a 5% increase was rejected, a 17% settlement was achieved following strike action. Importantly, the strikes spread amongst low paid workers in local government, such as the gravediggers of Liverpool, and in the health service where state employers made a more concerted attempt to keep increases within government guidelines. The myth of the 'winter of discontent' was created in a moral panic against the unions by the media and the Conservative opposition of the time. Labour was presented as failing in a growing crisis and of being tied to trade unions who were increasingly out of control.[15]

Box 2.4: *Conservative Employment and Trade Union Acts: 1980 to 1993*

Employment Act 1980
- Immunities removed from secondary action
- Picketing restricted to own place of work, with code of practice recommendation of limit of six pickets
- Restrictions on closed shop: requirement of ballot of workforce with 80% in favour for new agreements
- Government funds made available for union ballots
- Repeal of union recognition procedure

Employment Act 1982
- Further limitations on definition of a trade dispute, limiting to those wholly or mainly concerning immediate terms and conditions of employment, removing inter-union disputes (e.g. around demarcation) and political disputes, disputes with another employer than workers' own
- Further restrictions on closed shop with 80% ballot required in all cases every 5 years
- Compensation to employees dismissed because of closed shop Employers able to obtain injunctions against unions and claim damages
- Removal of 'union only' clauses in commercial agreements

1984 Trade Union Act
- Union election of officer's regulation introduced requiring executive ballots every five years
- Re-balloting on union political funds required every 10 years
- Secret ballot (postal or workplace) required before industrial action

Employment Act 1988
- Industrial action over closed shop loses immunity
- Outlawed dismissal for non-union membership
- Unlawful for unions to discipline members for not being involved in industrial action, courts empowered to award up to £30,000 for infringements

- Election necessary for all union offices
- Commissioner (CROTUM) established to assist members in legal action against unions
- Union finances open to inspection
- Unions prevented from paying members' or officials' fines

Employment Act 1989
- Tribunal changes
- Removal of gender and age restrictions
- Exemption of small employers from requiring discipline procedure
- Abolition of training commission

Employment Act 1990
- Abolition of pre-entry closed shop, unlawful to refuse employment on basis of non-union membership
- Unlawful to induce action from workers not party to the trade dispute (secondary action)
- Unions liable to any action by any officers in industrial action unless repudiation in writing.
- Industrial action in support of workers dismissed in unballoted action becomes illegal even if the action itself is balloted.
- Allowed selective dismissal of strikers

Trade Union and Labour Relations (Consolidation) Act 1992
- Consolidation of all trade union and employment law (Trade Union Act 2016 mainly a series of amendments to the 1992 Act)
- Brings together all collective trade union and employment rights, does not include individual rights
- Allows courts to ignore small, accidental, failures in conduct of industrial action ballots
- Restricts industrial action where there might be injury to persons or property

Trade Union Reform and Employment Rights Act 1993
- Changes in the constitution of Acas, statutory duty to promote collective bargaining removed.
- Postal ballot for industrial action with seven-day notice to employer

- Union members involved in industrial action ballot to be identified
- Individuals able to seek injunction against unlawful action
- Individuals free to join union of their own choice (abolition of Bridlington Agreement)
- Creation of Commission for Protection Against Unlawful Industrial Action
- Written consent required for 'check-off' of union subscriptions every three years
- Independent scrutiny of ballots
- Certification Officer extended powers to scrutinise union finances
- Postal ballot for union mergers
- Support for individual contracts
- Abolition of Wages Councils
- Introduction of European Commission measures on individual rights:
  o Increased maternity leave
  o Right to written statement of employment
  o Unlawful to dismiss health and safety representatives in the course of their duties and those walking off unsafe worksites
  o Right of individuals to challenge collective agreement in contravention of equal treatment terms
  o Changes to TUPE regulations
  o Changes to redundancy terms

Trade Unions Under Thatcher and Major

In the context of the 'social contract', and with inflation posed as the major threat to a market economy, the Conservative Party in opposition went through a substantial policy review. In what has been argued to be a 'pragmatic' move and one prompted by the International Monetary Fund (IMF) as a condition on a loan, Callaghan's Labour Government introduced monetarism in the form of cash limits on spending as the first step towards reducing state expenditure. Attached to this came limits to pay increases, and cuts in public spending. The Conservative Party proposed a more substantial rethink of policy, incorporating neoliberal economic theory into their policy making. Built on the primacy of the market, and a rolling back of the state, this would be a fundamental shift

71

in social and economic orthodoxy towards what would later be talked of as 'Thatcherism'. Neoliberalism was thrust into the mainstream. Trade unions were in the firing line in a broad redefining of proposed economic policy. Some argued that inflation itself was driven by the ability of militant trade unions to achieve 'unrealistic' wage demands. Others, and particularly the ideologues of the new Conservatism, argued that while not the cause of inflation, trade unions were a barrier to the necessary remedy which was cutting back public spending and expanding the 'free market' to replace the growing void in provision and services. Ironically, perhaps, this move towards support for market solutions led to an initial promotion of workplace based collective bargaining – at a time of state imposed wage restraint – in order to make 'collective bargaining a more orderly and responsible process.'[16]

While some neoliberal writers argued that the Thatcher trade union reforms were 'pragmatic rather than strategic'[17], there was clearly an underlying view of long-term and fundamental change in the position and nature of organised labour inherent in the proposals. Not only was this a move away from the political consensus of the previous quarter century – represented in industrial relations by a belief in voluntarism – it was also a move towards a far more explicit class politics from the Conservative Party in order to shift the balance of power between labour and capital decisively towards capital. Principally, the reforms attacked what the neoliberal thinkers driving them considered 'trade union monopoly practices': their ability to stage effective collective industrial action and the existence of closed shop agreements. The key underlying problem was, for them, trade union immunity, or, as Keith Joseph put it, their 'unique privileges.' These became the subject of an early Thatcher government Green Paper.[18] In a pamphlet written by Joseph, the key problem was identified as finding the cure for inflation. Inflation, or so the pamphlet claimed, was not caused by trade union power but trade union power would inhibit the necessary cure. In arguments echoing Peto and Hayek, Joseph argued that the power of unions would make the cure more difficult, giving them advantage in a class war:

'The reason why the 'Labour Movement' has been such a disaster for the people it professes to serve is that too many of its leaders have presented the movement as a war of liberation, a war between "good" socialism and "bad" capitalism. In the mistaken belief that free enterprise is "the class enemy", they have taught workers to resist efficiency, obstruct management, insist on over-manning, resent profit and ignore consumers.'[19]

Another underlying belief on which the reforms were based was that trade unions had fallen into the hands of a left wing, politically motivated leadership who manipulated or controlled a more moderate membership. Presented in 'class war' terms, this would be a long war of attrition: a long war involving both the tightening of trade union regulation alongside some pitched battles. As Charles Hanson of the Institute of Economic Affairs has presented it, the war involved:

> 'a series of steps building upon each other in a logical and indeed evolutionary manner. But the legislation would, of itself, have been insufficient. A successful confrontation with mindless militancy was the essential buttress.'[20]

There was a clear confrontation after 1979 which saw the tightening of trade union law after a series of bitter disputes. This increasingly had the appearance of a fight to the death for trade unions; most notably of course the eighteen-month strike by the National Union of Miners, a dispute which was portrayed by the Thatcher government as a war with 'the enemy within'. Thatcher was distancing herself from the Heath, who she felt had failed to confront the power of the unions and that of the NUM in particular.

In terms of industrial relations and trade union reform the Conservatives were clearly looking at attacking immunities but, reflecting on the failures of the *Industrial Relations Act* in 1971, this would be achieved through a steady erosion – a 'salami slicing' – rather than as a one-off reform (see Box 2.4). In the eighteen years of Conservative government, between 1979 and 1997, eight major Acts of Parliament were passed which constrained the action of trade unions. This includes the 1992 Act, which largely consolidated the measures and forms the basis on which the 2016 Act built. At the end of their term, in 1997, the Conservative Party still had ambitions to contain trade unions further as, in a Green Paper, they outlined their proposal to limit strikes further.

While these were separate pieces of legislation they can be considered together, as a cumulative and coherent attempt to unravel the protections gained by trade unions consistent with a drive towards a neoliberal utopia. At the end of the period of Conservative government in 1997, trade union action was clearly more constrained than in 1979. Immunity for strike action was increasingly restricted to immediate disputes between workers and their immediate employer, with a banning of secondary and political action. Industrial action, also, was required to be the result of a ballot of workers involved with notice given to the employer. This ruled out any spontaneous action by workers – wildcat strikes – as an immediate challenge or response. Picketing was restricted to the workers' own immediate place of work. The *Code of Practice* restricted the number of pickets at any workplace entrance, making mass pickets vulnerable to public order prosecution.

Central to the strategy was the gradual abolition of the closed shop where, through agreement with an employer, only trade union members were employed. For some closed shops, under pre-entry agreements, membership of a trade union was required before employment. This was often a means of restricting employment to workers who had completed an apprenticeship or similar training. In others, where membership was required after acceptance of employment, the closed shop was to protect from 'free riders' who might want the benefits that a trade union secured through collective bargaining but without the cost of actually joining a union. However, in the name of free choice and justified as a challenge to trade union monopoly practice, both pre- and post-entry closed shop agreements were gradually abolished. Legislation also abolished sectoral wage councils, which effectively determined a minimum wage in sectors where unionization was limited and collective bargaining weak. Unions were also progressively excluded from other state agencies concerned with economic and industrial development, as well as the training agencies concerned with the development and passing on of employment skills. With the idea that the trade unions needed to be liberated from a politically motivated leadership, legislation also established two Commissions: the Commission for the Rights of Trade Union Members (CROTUM), which was to assist members in proceedings against their own unions, and the Commission for Protection Against Industrial Action (CPAIA) with:

'the power to grant assistance to an individual who was an actual or prospective party to certain proceedings ... that a trade union had done, or was likely to do, [as] an unlawful act, and an effect of that act was to prevent or delay the supply of goods and services, or to reduce the quality of goods and services supplied to that individual, because of industrial action unlawfully organised by a trade union.'[21]

Both Commissions proved to have little work and were abolished as costly irrelevancies by the Blair government in 1999.

These developments came with the withdrawal of state support, and rapid decline, for much of Britain's traditional industry. Nationalised

74

industries were moved to the private sector or were allowed to fail. While the Conservative election campaign used the slogan 'Britain isn't working', relating to high levels of unemployment under Labour, the level began to shoot up after the election, rising from a rate of 5.3% in mid-1979 to a high of 11.8% in 1984. In the early 1980s, the UK, which had been 'the workshop of the world', became for the first time a net importer of manufactured goods.[22]

The first major impact of this attitude to nationalised industries came in 1979, with a pay claim in the steel industry. The claim was met by threats of major redundancies, a situation which escalated into a national strike.[23] Even more definitive was, of course, the miners' strike where the campaign against pit closures merged into a challenge to the new trade union laws. In a strategy which remains contentious for some commentators, the NUM refused to ballot its membership on the industrial action and had their funds sequestrated as a consequence, amongst other things, of the refusal to recognize the new law introduced the previous year. Rather than any attempt at resolution with the miners, the government were happy to see the dispute presented as a confrontation with the 'enemy within': having fought Argentina in the South Atlantic, Thatcher was now an open class warrior at home. Pitched battles were fought between a militarised police force and picketing miners. Most dramatically, in events still the subject of a fierce campaign, mounted police charged peaceful pickets at the Orgreave coke works. Media footage was doctored to twist events to make the police action appear a response to violence from the pickets. However, all charges against miners arrested at the picket were subsequently dropped, with supporters still pushing for an inquiry into the doctoring of police evidence.[24] During the strike pit villages were kept under siege by police.

The government's attitude to trade unions was also reflected in their decree that employment at the Government Communications

---

Box 2.5: *Trade Unions and Industrial Action 1996 (Conservative Government Green Paper)*

· Notice period for industrial action should be raised from 7 to 14 days
· Majority of those entitled to vote should be required for industrial action

Headquarters (GCHQ) – the secret communications centre – was incompatible with trade union membership as a matter of national security. This sparked major trade union de-recognition campaigns by employers in a number of industries, particularly in the newspaper industry, where there were major disputes and mass picketing in defense of skilled jobs, and the union closed shop saw a move – pioneered by *The Times*, owned by Rupert Murdoch – of national newspapers from Fleet Street to Wapping.

The claim that it was the 'Thatcher legislation' which was the immediate cause of a dramatic decline in industrial action is, however, not sustainable. Closure of highly unionised traditional industry with increasingly globalised production clearly had a place in this process, as did the rise in structural unemployment, in what proved a trend in all major industrial economies of the west. Again, reflecting more global changes, increasingly the locus of trade union membership switched from traditional industries to the public sector; militant workers were more likely teachers, civil servants or health workers and no longer the miner or car worker of previous times. The legislation was a means of surrounding the trade unions within increasingly tighter legislation, inhibiting any action by workers via the organisations through which they had a voice in the workplace and wider society. While unofficial actions were squeezed out, more by the undermining of workplace organisation than by legislation itself, the unions themselves became more strategic in their use of industrial action.

The Conservatives were not finished with attempting to legislate to limit trade union action. In 1996, as an indicator of potential action and in preparation for the imminent election, the Conservatives produced a green paper (see Box 2.5) arguing that they would raise the majority required and extend notice period for industrial action.[25]

The move wasn't totally in one direction. To some extent trade unions began to recognise an institution that might help protect employment rights and provide a role for trade unionism. In the 1980s and 1990s the European Community increasingly played an important role in maintaining employment rights. Rather reluctantly, the Conservatives brought some of these into UK legislation. Following an address by Jacques Delors, President of the European Commission, at the TUC in 1988 where he stressed his social vision of Europe, the unions tended to move towards support for its institutions. The EU was presented, at least in part, as a means to protect working conditions and perhaps advance employee voice in a domestic environment where these were under attack. The main initial victory was better protection for workers who had been moved from public to private sector employment in the rush to contract-out and privatise services promoted by the Thatcher government. Already low paid, workers found their conditions worsened when they were moved from direct employment with local authorities or the NHS to agencies contracting for the work. Public sector unions campaigned through appeal to European regulation – in this case the *Acquired Rights Directive* 1977 – to present the case that in transfer, the workers should keep their initial terms and conditions of employment. Finally, the Directive was brought into UK law as the *Transfer of Undertakings (Protection of Employment)* or TUPE Regulations, which helped numerous workers in the increasingly frequent transfers of employment due to privatisation and other takeovers of ownership. The EU was predominantly posing policy in terms of the involvement of 'stakeholders' – and thus trying to draw in trade unions and other parties. The UK was increasingly fixated with shareholder values, that is a return on capital as the measure of health in the economy. The Conservatives objected to the increasingly social vision of the EU, epitomised by the *Social Chapter* (or Protocol on Social Policy annexed to the Treaty EU) of the *Maastricht Treaty*. This attempted to address and harmonise member states on issues of equal opportunities, working conditions, and other employment rights. This was not directly concerned with pay or trade union rights. While the UK excluded itself from regulations on employee consultation within companies operating across more than one EU member state, many such companies complied with the regulation and established European Works Councils. Importantly, also, the EU established regulations and minimum standards in the areas not just of human rights but also around health and safety at work. As we shall see, under the auspices of health and safety came the regulation of working hours, the *Working Time Directive*, which became a particular bogey for neoliberals. The dominant policy ethos of the EU and of the UK were diverging. The EU also went through a period of expansion with the accession of Eastern European states following the collapse of the USSR. With this came tensions over the free movement of labour with jobs in the UK, often casual and low paid, becoming open to migrant workers from Poland, Latvia and other accession states.

Fairness at Work? The Labour Government 1997-2010

'The essential elements of the trade union legislation of the 1980s will remain. There will be no return to secondary action, flying pickets, strikes without ballots, the closed shop and all the rest. The changes that we do propose would leave British law the most restrictive on trade unions in the Western world.' Tony Blair[26]

In the shift to 'New Labour' under the leadership of Tony Blair, one key change was a distancing of the Labour Party from the trade unions. The 'New Labour' government, while adamant that it would not repeal or reverse any of the constraints on unions introduced by the Thatcher government, proposed to incorporate EU regulation arising from signing the Social Chapter, and to establish minimum standards in both individual and collective employment rights. Most significant was the introduction of a national minimum wage (NMW), promised in their election manifesto (see Box 2.6). In part, this reversed the abolition of wages councils in 1993[27,] which had operated where trade unions tended to be weak. The introduction of the NMW also indicated how weak collective bargaining had become. The NMW was not constructed to meet the subsistence needs of those in low pay employment, rather the level was determined by the Low Pay Commission in terms of limited impact on employment, employer cost, and particularly the welfare budget. This deliberately limited employers' labour costs, with the requirement to meet the actual cost of living for the low paid falling with the Exchequer and the benefit system, not their employer. The minimum cost of living requirement for those in employment would be met by the benefit system, through tax credits, rather than as additional labour costs to an employer. William Brown, an initial member of the Low Pay

Box 2.6: *National Minimum Wage Act 1998*

- National minimum wage for over 21s
- 'training rate' applicable for those aged below 21
- Exemption for volunteer work, residents in charities and religious communities
- Low Pay Commission to recommend minimum rate changes and coverage

Commission, the body established to set the level of the NMW, was to comment that:

> 'the Commission's terms of reference studiously avoided any suggestion that the minimum wage should be set at a level to represent some sort of acceptable living standard. An important fiscal motivation for a statutory minimum wage was the fact that, without any floor to wages, ever more low-paid employees with families were becoming entitled to means-tested in-work benefits, at ever-increasing cost to the Exchequer. The benefits system was in effect subsidising low-paying employers.'[28]

So, as Brown indicates, the government objective was to move the jobless into work, with the benefit system, working tax credits, subsidising low paying employers.

The nature of employee voice was also changed, with the incorporation of the *Social Chapter*. The EU had already adopted a Directive, referred to as the *European Works Council Directive*,[29] requiring employers to inform and consult with employees in companies with bases in more than one EU member country. While employers should inform and consult employee representatives on major strategic decisions, this did not inhibit major plant closures and redundancies – the main issues that this was intended to address in the UK. These remained problematic, as with the sale of Rover cars in the UK by their owners BMW. As we have seen, in accordance with co-determination laws, private companies in Germany are required to establish a works council, elected by and from the workforce, with the rights to be consulted and to challenge a range of management decisions impacting the workplace. Trade unions, in a 'dual system', remain concerned with collective bargaining across industries and companies, and do this in consultation with the works councils. Representation on the works council, anyway, tends to be drawn from trade unions which present a slate of candidates in the election. The main company decisions body is the supervisory board which also has equal representation from management and workers.

In 2002 the EU introduced a *Directive for Information and Consultation* (ICE)[30] in the context of complaints that the UK system offered no facility for consultation over redundancy in workplaces where unions were not recognised. Unlike other countries, at least before the new accession countries of Eastern Europe, the UK retained the only industrial relations

Box 2.7: *1998 Working Time Regulations*

• Implements EC Directive with respect to maximum working hours
• Does not apply to specified sectors including air, rail, road and sea, armed forces and police
• A limit of average 48 hours working week, with possible opt-out
• Daily and weekly rest entitlements and rest breaks
• A right to 4 weeks paid annual leave and to be paid for accrued but untaken leave on termination of employment
• Special provisions relating to night work

system which did not have some form of employee consultation system – of 'works councils' – even if without the rights established in German co-determination. While the UK measures to comply with the ICE regulations recognised pre-existing arrangements, the regulation deliberately did not specify trade union representation or even involvement in consultation.[31]

Researchers for the 2004 Workplace Employment Relations Survey (WERS) could observe from their long-term results that:

> Whereas the *raison d'être* of union representative structures was historically that of acting as a mechanism for negotiations to take place between managers and representatives, the focus of many new representative structures is that of 'consultation' with employees, whereby managers seek employees' views, via representatives, as part of the management decision making process.[32]

An optimistic view was that such mechanisms could be used to enhance independent employee voice and strengthen union presence. Some looked to systems like the works councils in Germany, part of a broader co-determination which incorporates the unions within the institutional arrangements of capital,[33] as a direction for the UK. The TUC, in the context of an exploration of company arrangements in Sweden, France and Germany, advocated a strengthening of the ICE arrangements in the UK as 'part of the solution to delivering an economy with higher skills, investment and overall performance as a means to underpin strong and sustainable future growth.'[34] However, there was a recognition by the TUC that such an enhancement of ICE arrangements might be at 'risk of marginalisation of unions.'[35] There is evidence that, in contrast to

Germany where a system of works councils were established in part to undermine a militant labour movement, and the unions could essentially colonise them from a position of strength in the 1950s and 1960s, in the UK employers have been using consultation arrangements as a means of undermining existing trade union agreements and of avoiding pressures for recognition.[36]

As part of incorporating the *Social Chapter* the government introduced the Working Time Directive into UK legislation (see Box 2.7). Under the auspices of health and safety at work the directive sought control over 'minimum periods of daily rest, weekly rest and annual leave, to breaks and maximum weekly working time'[37] as well as aspects of night work, shift work and the patterns of work. The key objective was to regulate to ensure that 'the average working time for each seven-day period, including overtime, does not exceed 48 hours.' A range of occupations were exempted in the UK regulations, allowing an employer to ask employees to sign an 'opt-out'. In the name of 'flexibility' the UK

Box 2.8: *1999 Employment Relations Act*

• Recognition and negotiation procedures for employers with at least 21 workers, establishment of bargaining unit
• Derecognition from loss of trade union independence or majority support of bargaining unit
• Complaint process for use of political funds and breach of union disciplinary, electoral or other internal rules
• Dismissal for participation in official industrial action deemed unfair within a protected period of 8 weeks
• Ballot and notice provisions for strike or industrial action
• Employee permitted to bring companion to any hearing
• Part-time workers to be treated no less favourably
• Abolishes offices of Commissioner for Rights of Trade Union Members and Commissioner for Protection Against Unlawful Industrial Action
• Funds to be provided to assist in developing employment partnerships
• Regulation of employment agencies
• Regulation with respect to treatment of employees in transfer of undertakings (EC) TUPE

---

remained a long-hours working culture where other European countries attempted to move towards a 35-hour week.

In 1998, the 'New Labour' government introduced *Fairness at Work*, its White Paper on trade union and employment rights reform. In his forward, Tony Blair was clear that this would not involve any repeal of the Thatcher government's measures:

> The days of strikes without ballots, mass picketing, closed shops and secondary action are over. Even after the changes we propose, Britain will have the most lightly regulated labour market of any leading economy in the world. But it cannot be just to deny British citizens basic canons of fairness - rights to claim unfair dismissal, rights against discrimination for making a free choice of being a union member, rights to unpaid parental leave - that are a matter of course elsewhere.[38]

The 1999 *Employment Relations Act*, (see Box 2.8) the eventual Labour legislation arising from consultation on their White Paper, introduced the Blair government's measures for employment relations and trade union reform. Centrally, there was a procedure for trade union recognition, supposedly automatically if more than half the 'bargaining unit' were members of a trade union, or through a ballot if more than ten per-cent of the relevant workforce requested it. As a gesture in this direction the incoming government had reversed the decision to derecognise unions at GCHQ. They now proposed a procedure where a workforce could, under defined conditions, ask for a ballot to establish collective bargaining with an independent union. The Act contained changes to discipline and grievance procedure, specifically allowing employees representation within any meetings with management. It also contained improvements to parental leave and individual rights. The White Paper also opened discussion on the deterioration of terms of employment that were taking place, often in the name of increased flexibility. The paper certainly didn't challenge the new individualism in employment; for example, while it noted the increased use of 'zero hours' contracts, there was no criticism, let alone alleviation. The objective was to maintain flexibility in the labour market and in working practices.

The Coalition, the State of the Unions, and the Carr Review

Issues of industrial relations moved into the background, barring the occasional dispute where there was a public impact. This of course did not mean that employment conflicts had ended. Instead of a collective response, the kind of public strike which could hit the media, responses to problems tended to be private and individual. In the new and unorganised workplace, such as the call centres that replaced the factories as the sites of mass employment, workers with problems prove more likely to try to move job – or just leave – rather than lodge a complaint, especially when complaining is likely to prompt dismissal. Perhaps half of employees have direct experience of bullying,[39] and, by the turn of the 21st century workplace bullying had become endemic. With the growing insecurity of the labour market, rather than complain about conditions or management behaviour through individual or collective representation, workers resorted to quitting the job. In the words of commentators on the labour market, workers resort to 'exit' rather than 'voice'.[40] Increasingly, the UK moved towards the neoliberal ideal of a labour market of the self-employed.[41]

As the number of strikes declined, some workplace conflicts were brought into the tribunal system. The government attempted to contain this through tightening access to judicial resolution to employment problems, such as: sex, disability or racial discrimination; unfair dismissal; breach of employment contract; unfair wage deductions; etc., which are the jurisdiction of employment tribunals. The Cameron government's solution, justified in terms of austerity measures and cuts to the budget of the Justice Department, was to introduce fees for taking cases. The inevitable and deliberate result of a charge of between £400 and £1200 to take a claim, was a substantial reduction in the number of cases brought. A report by the Ministry of Justice on the introduction of fees for employment tribunals argues that the policy has been a success because it reduced the number of actions by almost 70%.[42] However, as commentators have observed, 'for a worker who has been ripped off for £1,000 worth of wages and holiday pay, risking £400 to go to tribunal is just throwing good money after bad.'[43] As was the government's original intention, the policy managed to price workers out of voicing employment problems. Claims on grounds of discrimination on sexual orientation alone reduced by over 70 per cent.[44] In July 2017, however, following a challenge to these fees brought by Unison, citing law going back to the Magna Carta, the Supreme Court ruled that the fees were unlawful and that their introduction 'has the effect of preventing access to justice.' The ruling stated that:

'the evidence before the Court shows that the effect of the Fees Order was a dramatic and persistent fall in the number of claims brought in ETs, with a greater fall in the number of lower value claims and claims in which a financial remedy was not sought. Fees were the most frequently cited reason for not submitting a claim.'[45]

Since they were judged unlawful, it is also likely that much of the £32 million paid in fees will have to be reimbursed to those who brought cases. Many of these will have been funded by trade unions in cases brought on behalf their members. However, excluded are those who did not take legitimate cases because of the prohibitive cost of such an action.

While much reduced, the government still faced industrial disputes which they found to be a major irritant, particularly in terms of the tactics adopted by workers. Representation of workers has, to a limited extent, been via redirection and rechannelling. To some extent the shop steward role is being carried out by the Citizens' Advice Bureau,[46] although this has been limited by CAB's own escalating workload and limited resources, compounded by a clientele worried by the benefit crisis and individual debt.

In absolute terms the decline of trade unionism in Britain can be seen in membership figures (see Box 2.9). Having hit a peak in 1979 at 13.2 million, the last reported membership figure has fallen to 6.5 million. The one consolation might be that this decline now appears to have plateaued.[47] However, one of the most significant changes in trade union membership since its peak has been a move from the private to public sector. Continued reduction in membership in the private sector is masked by growth in public sector membership. Not only are trade unions increasingly representing public sector workers, membership is increasingly female. As the 2016 statistical report notes:

'female employees are more likely to be a trade union member. 55% of union members were female in 2015, up from 45% in 1995. The proportion of female employees who were in a trade union was around 27.7% in 2015, unchanged from 2014. In comparison, 21.7% of male employees were in a trade union in 2015, down from 22.3% in 2014.'[48]

One of the changes in the labour market behind these shifts is the collapse of traditional industries – the previous masculine bulwarks of trade unionism – replaced by public sector employment. The two industrial sectors with highest union membership density of over 50%, are public administration and education. These are followed, with over 40% trade union density, by health and social care, and electricity and gas supply, being public sector or formally so.[49]

Employment has increasingly become casual and part-time. A recent analysis of official labour market statistics by the TUC indicates that only one in forty new jobs created in the UK between 2008 and 2014 are full-time.[50] The disappearance of secure and full-time employment has created insecurity and undermined the continuity of trade union regeneration, with 'employees with ten or more years of service making up about 52% of all union members but only 31 per cent of employees.'[51]

Not only are trade union members likely to have had longevity of employment, they are far more likely to be older, with 37% of members over the age of 50. With an increasingly ageing membership the unions have a constant need to recruit just to replace member retirements; younger workers are less likely to join unions than older. As employment is becoming less secure so is union membership. With frequent changes of employment comes at best sporadic union membership, which inhibits any concerted campaigns or workplace organisation. Union membership campaigns falter, as workplace activists move on. Even with tighter labour markets, 'exit' is the most likely way for workers, particularly the young, to deal with problems at work.

Trade unions themselves have changed in the last few decades. The absolute number of trade unions has reduced quite dramatically, from 502 in 1983 to just 160 in 2015.[52] Of these, fifty are members of the TUC. But this masks some other changes. On one side, there is the folding of some craft unions representing a niche, whose membership cannot be sustained because of disappearing trades and occupations, sometimes quite localised: the Church and Oswaldwistle Power-Loom Overseers Society, as well as the Engineering and Fasteners Trade Union were but two ceasing registration in the recent period. Some of the decline in trade union membership must be attributed to the collapse of traditional industries. Almost the smallest member union of the TUC is now the NUM, having once boasted over a quarter of a million members in 1980, it now has an overall membership of around 1,250.[53] The National Association of Colliery Overmen, Deputies and Shotfirers (NACODS)

Box 2.9: *Trade union membership levels in the UK from 1892 to*

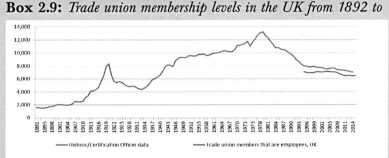

2015

From: BIS, *Trade Union Membership: Statistical Bulletin,* May 2016

had a membership of over 19,000 in 1980 but by 2014 was the smallest TUC union, down to only 286 members, and ceased existance the following year.[54] The British Association of Colliery Management, the majority of whose members were 'retired', also disappeared into a merger in late 2014.

The main decline in the number of trade unions was because of such mergers. This is creating larger blocks dominated by two unions: Unite, with a majority male membership within the private sector, and Unison, with a more female and public sector membership. Each have over 1.3 million members and together constitute more than a third of overall trade unionists. Following in size is the other main general union, the GMBU, with over 600,000 members, then the shop workers' union USDAW, then the two teachers unions: the National Union of Teachers, which itself merged with the Association of Teachers and Lecturers (ATL) in 2017 to form the National Education Union (NEU), and the National Association of Schoolmasters and Union of Women Teachers (NASUWT), formed of a past merger.[55] Not yet within the TUC are a number of new unions, often focused around particular disputes and short lived as a result. Some exceptions to these 'pop-up' unions are the Industrial Workers of the World (IWW) and the Independent Workers of Great Britain. Registering first in 2006, with 163 members and growing to 750 in 2015, the IWW traces its ancestry to organisers of unskilled workers in the early 20th century, predominantly in the USA but also promoting the 'one big union' in the UK. Most notable amongst their reference points is a strike in Clydeside by Singer Sewing Machine workers who faced new scientific management and mass production methods moving to Scotland.[56] The IWGB is based in London and has built its membership to 810. Founded amongst workers employed by cleaning agencies but spreading now to cycle delivery riders, foster carers, and others in the precarious, low pay economy. Other unions appear and disappear, such as the appropriately named 'Pop Up' union which formed amongst staff at Sussex University around a specific dispute.[57] It is, as yet, unclear whether these herald a new wave of unionisation, predominantly amongst the low paid, and largely outside of the established institutions and practices. It is clear that some overlap exists between these new unions and general unions in the attempt to recruit and organise amongst the low paid. The very insecurity of casual – often agency – working poses new problems.

Starting in the 1980s in the USA, the 'Justice for Janitors' campaign saw the Service Employees International Union (SEIU) organising low paid – and often vulnerable – immigrant workers protesting low pay and poor conditions of contract cleaning. Contracting out had created an often-invisible stratum of workers engaged in cleaning and other facility services.[58] The workers suffered from low pay and poor conditions, squeezed by contractors continually cutting costs in a 'race to the bottom'.

Soon, a similar campaign was established in the UK, *Justice for Cleaners*, organised initially by the Transport and General Workers Union (TGWU), a precursor union to Unite. Around the same time the London Living Wage Campaign was established by a collection of trade unions, churches, and academics, as well as community groups. Rather than the minimum wage, which, while staunching absolute low wages, still often needed supplementing with welfare benefits to reach subsistence level, the London group proposed a 'Living Wage' which would provide for at least the basic cost of living. A 2001 report for the campaign puts the London living wage at £6.30 an hour when the minimum wage was then set at £3.70.[59] There emerged, however, a rift between the traditional pattern of trade union bargaining accepting concessions in a compromise and the expectations and ambitions of the new membership, who:

'weren't grateful for their 'living wage' when it meant they paid for it in reduced hours, and had to work with fewer employers, while working more intensely. They took action without permission and didn't do what they were told.'[60]

Some low paid workers, often working for cleaning contractors but also others, turned to the IWW or the IWGB.[61] High profile campaigns around the Living Wage were staged against cleaning contractors at the John Lewis Partnership's flagship store in Oxford Street, where the IWGB organised its first, successful, industrial action ballot.

The Cameron government, in a surprise move, took up the basis of this campaign in an attempt both to appropriate it and defuse action around the minimum wage, action which also intended to reduce in-work benefits. But, of course, alongside the apparent concession on wages – which bypassed any trade union or bargaining structures – came a clampdown on action which might be used to further the organisation of these low paid workers. Before considering this more fully, a brief consideration of the decline in industrial action and other ways that workplace discontent was being expressed, will be useful.

A reduction in union membership and industrial action has been a feature of most Western industrial societies, at least those where neo-liberal policies became dominant and the Thatcher Governments' legislation impacted on the level of industrial disputes, although not in a clear-cut way. Since the 1970s, and prior to legislation, the UK has seen a dramatic decline in the official conflict count. In 1970 there were 3,906 disputes in progress, the highest recorded number, although 1972 saw the highest number of working days lost at around 23 million. According to the recent official report: '[t]he 2015 working days lost total (170,000) is not only lower than the total last year, but is the second lowest annual total since records began in 1891 (the lowest was 157,000 in 2005).'[62]

Big fluctuations can occur, with 30 million days lost in 1979 principally accounted for by the public-sector disputes, the 'winter of discontent', while 27 million days in 1984 are accounted for by the miners' strike (See Box 2.10). Changes between 2012 and 2013 are caused by just one major dispute, as the current report notes:

'Once again education has been the sector with the largest number of working days lost, accounting for just under 50% of the working days lost in 2013. However, this industrial group only accounted for 25% of all strikes (28), indicating that the number of workers taking part in these strikes is, on average, greater than other industrial groups. The second largest number of working days lost was public administration and defence, with 180,200 days lost in 2013, accounting for a further 41% of the working days lost.'[63]

Box 2.10: *Working days lost (WDL), UK, 1891 to 2015*
From: ONS Labour Disputes in the UK: 2015

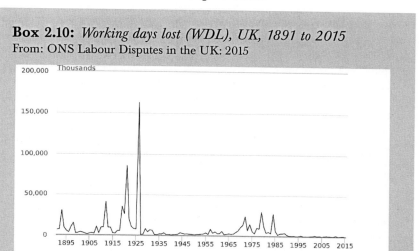

But this absolute decline in recorded industrial action might mask other changes in employment relations. In years with the highest number of recorded disputes there were two features that seemed to plague management and the policy makers: unofficial disputes and the activities of shop stewards. As the most authoritative text book of the period put it:

'For several recent years the Department has distinguished between official strikes and unofficial strikes, the latter being strikes which have not been sanctioned by the appropriate union authority. Their figures show that over 95 per cent of strikes during 1964-6 were unofficial, and only about 3 per cent official. The official strikes, however, account for 30 per cent of the working days lost.'[64]

What has disappeared from these figures are unofficial strike actions, happening almost spontaneously and under the control of the shop-floor worker and their immediate representatives rather than trade union officials. The remaining use of the strike weapon, more robustly under the control of trade union bureaucracy, appears to be deployed far more 'strategically', as periodic 'one day' rather than 'all out' actions. To a limited extent, the decline might also be related to middle managers not reporting incidents of unofficial and spontaneous industrial action and short stoppages in the workplace. In the past it might have been advantageous for middle management to pass any dispute up the hierarchy but, with the delayering and delegation which came to management approaches in the 1980s, such reporting became increasingly frowned upon.[65] More significantly, of course, and a key objective of the 1980s legislation, was the attack on shop stewards and workplace representation.

The ideological foundation for the attack on shop stewards was based around the assumption that employee representatives were the cause of workplace conflict. Rather than being viewed as the people who give conflict a 'voice' and, importantly, seek some resolution with management through representation, representatives are considered to be the major factor in conflicts. Conflict might escalate into some form of express action if management does not listen to the complaints and seek resolution. In squeezing out workplace representatives, and perhaps the spontaneous dispute, conflict finds alternative expression, even if this is in an increased incidence of quitting and the heightened labour turnover already pointed to. Within the move towards neoliberalism, along with the marginalisation of employee voice, came the 'right to manage' or 'macho management' as it was often termed. If the symptom of this for individuals is the growing workplace bullying epidemic, then the collective symptom is management by diktat, with management refusing any meaningful bargaining with worker representatives.

The introduction of industrial action ballots allows an interesting comparison here. The table in Box 2.11 compares the number of strikes between 2002 and 2015 with the ballots calling for strike action in the same years. Two points can be made from the data. Firstly, the overwhelming number of strike ballots were in favour of taking action. In 2015, for instance, 503 ballots were held which supported strike action, although only 106 strikes resulted. This does not include the percentage of members taking part in the ballot or the percentage vote in favour – issues which will become important with the 2016 Act. Secondly – and as we have seen – only a relatively small proportion of ballots calling for strike action result in actual strike action. There are, of course, two possible reasons for this difference: while members might vote for industrial action, such action is not sanctioned by union staff. This would run counter to any argument – at the root of the neoliberal approach – that these officers were, for political motives, promoting strike action by members. If anything, the reverse is happening, and such officers often seek a means to avoid strike action. The other explanation, therefore, is

Box 2.11: *Industrial Action Ballots and the Number of Strikes 2002 to 2015*

	Ballots voting for strike action	Total no. of ballots	Strikes
2002	613	806	146
2003	684	899	133
2004	746	952	130
2005	663	815	116
2005	1094	1341	158
2007	637	767	142
2008	658	834	144
2009	458	579	98
2010	487	579	92
2011	903	994	149
2012	487	601	131
2013	417	494	114
2014	550	650	155
2015	503	568	106

that the show of support for action through the ballot – the sign of intention by the workers involved in dispute – prompts management into bargaining and attempting to resolve the grievances involved. Such ballots must be seen as part of the bargaining process, not as a hindrance to it. This, of course, needs to be considered in respect to the importance – and place – of industrial action ballots in the *Trade Union Act 2016*, rooted as it is in neoliberal ideology.

Despite the continued low level of strike action it has remained a fixation for the Conservatives. In November 2013, as Parliament was discussing the supposed 'so-called leverage tactics of Unite in the Grangemouth dispute'[66] David Cameron announced an inquiry into 'this sort of industrial intimidation' – with direct accusations against Len McClusky, the General Secretary of Unite – to be chaired by Bruce Carr QC. This was supposedly to be conducted along with representatives from the CBI and TUC, although ultimately without either. The terms of reference for this review were to be:

- alleged use of extreme tactics in industrial disputes, including so-called 'leverage' tactics; and the
- effectiveness of the existing legal framework to prevent inappropriate or intimidatory actions in Trade Disputes.[67]

Of course, the first question was over the actual meaning of 'leverage' in the context of any Unite campaign. The union, the target of Cameron, Conservative MPs, as well as much of the press, was itself quite clear on the tactic and its organising objective:

> 'Leverage is not a call for unofficial action. Leverage is about the democratic right of the Union to ensure that immoral employers cannot hide behind veils of secrecy and must conduct their business in an open and transparent fashion and accept the consequences of the moral judgements that may follow. It is in no way a replacement for collective strength. The development of industrial power remains vital if workers are to have the ability to win long-term. Leverage does not offer a solution that excludes the critical need to organise workers.'[68]

This was given a far more sinister spin by its opponents who claimed that Unite was engaged in the promotion of 'extreme tactics'. In practice, Carr utilised the list of disputes cited on the Unite web site, at least initially, to compile its own list of disputes which had been subject to such 'leverage' – dismissing the cases at Honda, where the union had won perhaps the most significant recognition agreement under the 1999 *Employment Relations Act*. The Review identified the disputes at INEOS, at the Grangemouth Chemicals and Refinery plant, London Underground Limited and Transport for London, Fire and Rescue Services disputes, Cleaners' disputes (principally at University of London), Total Lindsey Oil Refinery, the BESNA dispute on London Cross-Rail, London Buses, and Howdens Joinery dispute. What unites these disputes is not just their occurrence in the period of the inquiry but that most were relatively protracted. The disputes also involved a chain of contractors and subcontractors, each of them often tightening terms and conditions of service down the chain such as pressing for reductions in pay for already low paid workers.

Despite the list of disputes, some of which received considerable press coverage concerning the practices of the strikers, the Review found little which they could identify as substantial cases of the use of 'extreme tactics'. As well as conventional picketing, the use of new media in organising was studied. Evidence cited by the review, consisted of web pages, videos, and photographs posted by strikers themselves. One instance, evidenced by a YouTube video, showed:

> 'the protesters dancing, playing music, blowing horns whilst located on the road and pavement. There appears to be a bus which is unable to pass the protesters.'

Flash mobs like this were organised away from the immediate workplace of the strikers, or by supporters. In another instance, in support of cleaners at the University of London:

> 'students entered the Senate House adorned with beach towels, snorkels, and panama hats, playing Calypso music through the corridors of the building to protest about holiday provision for outsourced workers.'

The complaint seems to be that such tactics occur away from the immediate site of the conflict, with strikers and their supporters using such protest tactics as public displays. Some consternation related to 'Scabby the rat', an inflatable plastic rat, used by Crossrail workers protesting the use of blacklisting. 'Scabby' also appeared in the dispute by London bus drivers over payments during the Olympic Games. During a 'flash mob' organised outside a formal dinner attended by contractors, 'Scabby' joined in.

A superficially more substantial accusation against strikers, this time in a formal picket, was intimidation and the drinking of alcohol. This accusation was reported to Carr by Transport for London managers, who claimed:

> 'the atmosphere and conduct of picket lines [is] sometimes ... intimidating to non-striking staff and potentially customers. They cite the example of alcohol being consumed by a picket outside the Seven Sisters Depot. Pictures of the event are available on the 'RMT London Calling' website ...'[69]

The nearest that any of the photographs cited as evidence show of such activities are the union branch chair and regional officer 'enjoying the sun' by a table containing bottled water, some coffee cups, as well as some sauce bottles – clearly the remains of lunch. No sign of alcohol. Even Carr comments that 'it is not clear from these pictures that alcohol was consumed.'

Because the TUC had the well founded view that the Carr Review was a 'party political stunt', no affiliated union took any part in the proceedings. As Frances O'Grady, the TUC General Secretary, wrote to Bruce Carr:

'We are not aware of any trade union using 'extreme tactics' in any industrial dispute. Unions in dispute with employers have and will continue to use all and every legally compliant means of persuading the employer to take a different course of action.'[70]

Making the point that:

'The current legal framework governing the conduct of trade unions during trade disputes is among the toughest in any democratic state. Unions cannot take industrial action without complying with a series of requirements, including notices to the employer in a prescribed manner and postal ballots of all those being asked to withdraw their labour.'

There is little, therefore, which could support employer claims of intimidation – union 'leverage' – although some YouTube clips of singing, dancing, and the joy of collective action were placed in evidence. What concerned critics, including the TUC, was that the Carr Review ruled consideration of employer blacklists outside its terms of reference. This ruled out consideration of an important form of intimidation used by employers and the very issue central in at least one of the disputes more generally under consideration by Carr. The main reasons why the disputes considered by Carr were protracted, and caused considerable bitterness, was the intransigence of management. The development of neoliberalism has not just involved the fundamentals of share-holder values, but also the absolute prerogative of management. Despite the notions of 'market capitalism', management see bargaining between buyer and seller of labour power as anathema.

The framework of UK industrial relations, and the position of trade unions, was established around the turn of the 20th century, based on immunity to civil action for damages by another party when the union was engaged in a trade dispute. This didn't put them outside or above the law despite neoliberal claims, and what could constitute a trade dispute was left open. Following some abortive attempts at reform, by both Labour and Conservative governments, the Thatcher and Major governments of the 1980s and 1990s introduced a series of 'salami slicing' legislations which cut away at trade unions. These considerably limited the definition of a trade dispute, ruling out any sympathy or secondary action, narrowing it to workers and their immediate workplace. The changes also required the industrial action ballot to be held before immunities applied. Reflecting the neoliberal roots of these reforms, and the direct influence of Frederik Hayek, there was also the drive to attack the so-called 'monopoly powers' of trade unions. The reforms saw the end of closed shop agreements through a progressive tightening of legislation; outlawing collective bargaining agreements between employers and unions, which regulated the training and skills of the workforce through apprenticeship as qualification for union membership, and importantly stopped the 'freeloading' of workers, who gained the benefits of improved pay and conditions fought by unions and their members without themselves being members.

The other symbol of trade union monopoly for the Thatcherites, the picket line, still survived the onslaught but was seriously dented. With a few exceptions, principally around some of the so-called leverage actions, mass picketing symbolised by Grunwick, Orgreave during the miner's strike, and elsewhere, had ended. Perhaps nothing represents the fundamental difference between the individualism of neoliberalism and the collectivism of trade unionism than the attitude towards the picket line. For one, the very existance of the picket line is gross intimidation, with non-strikers who crossed the picket-line being considered heroic. For the other, nothing is more sacred in collective solidarity than the imperative of never crossing.

While the number of strikes had reduced dramatically since the 1980s, this was not considered enough. Strikes remained an irritant, a vestigial 'servant problem', which disrupted the supposed harmony of the economy. The trade unions had been corralled, but remained capable of action that impacted on others. Especially in the public sector, macho management alongside privatisation had done little to stifle the ability of trade unions to challenge autocracy and bullying. The proposal to limit the capacity of public sector unions to call strike action had long been part of Conservative ideology, and was tabled in party proposals in 1996, just before they lost office to Blair.

Already contained by the Acts of the 1980s and 1990s, unaffected by the Blair government, the unions were to be squeezed progressively tighter: the unions were 'kettled' by further reforms. While, as we shall see in the next section, this situation is presented as 'modernising' the law on trade unions it is, in fact, an attempt to reverse the reforms put in place since in the early 20th century. The aim has been a return to the conditions that prevailed with the Taff Vale judgement which crippled the trade unions for supposed intimidation of strike-breakers. While the withdrawal of labour may remain legal, almost anything associated with industrial action might then become defined as intimidation. Perhaps, with the casualisation of employment, we are reaching the neoliberal ideal: that while workers would have the right to strike, employers should have the right to replace them. An important change in the Conservative government's proposals in 2016 was to repeal regulation prohibiting the use of strikebreaking agency workers. The next section considers the proposals in the *Trade Union Bill* 2015, after the election of the Cameron government, and how it emerged as the 2016 Act.

Notes

1. Report of the *Royal Commission on Trade Unions and Employers Associations* (HMSO, 1968), Cmmn 3623
2. Paul Foot, "The Seamen's Struggle," in *The Incompatibles: trade union militancy and the consensus*, ed. Robin Blackburn and Alexander Cockburn (Harmondsworth: Penguin, in association with *New Left Review*, 1967), p.169-209. One of these men was John Prescott, at the time an official of the National Union of Seamen and author of the pamphlet *Not Wanted of Voyage*, a defence of the seaman's action which is drawn on by Foot's article
3. Barbara Castle, memorandum on Industrial Policy with attached *In Place of Strife* (1969); available from http://discovery.nationalarchives.gov.uk/details/addtobasket/D7660873 #imageViewerLink
4. See Jock Bruce-Gardyne, *Whatever Happened to the Quite Revolution? the Story of a Brave Experiment in Government* (London: Charles Knight & Co Ltd, 1974)
5. See Andrew Gamble, *The Free Economy and the Strong State: The Politics of Thatcherism* (Basingstoke and London: Macmillan, 1988)
6. Fair Deal at Work, *The Conservative approach to modern industrial relations*, published by the Conservative Political Centre, C.P.C. No. 400, April 1968
7. For a list of possible unfair practices under the Act see John Elliott, *Industrial Relations: The New Act* (London: *Financial Times*, 1971)
8. *Industrial Relations Act*, para 1(1)

9. See Ken Coates, *Work-Ins, Sit-Ins and Industrial Democracy* (Nottingham: Spokesman, 1981), and Alan Tuckman, "Workers' Control and the Politics of Factory Occupation in Britain in the 1970s," in *Ours to Master and to Own: Workers' Control from the Commune to the Present,* ed. Immanual Ness and Dario Azzellini (Chicago: Haymarket Books, 2011), p. 284-301

10. John Hughes, *A Special Case? Social Justice and the Miners* (Harmondsworth: Penguin, 1972)

11. *Employment Protection Act* 1975, para 17(1)

12. Ibid para 57(1)

13. Alan Bullock (Bullock Report), *Report of the Committee of Inquiry on Industrial Democracy,* vol. 6706 (HM Stationery Office, 1977) p.v para 1

14. Ibid, p. 171, para 9

15. Tara Martin López, *The Winter of Discontent: Myth, Memory, and History* (Liverpool University Press, 2014)

16. *The Right Approach* (Conservative policy statement, Oct 1976), available at: http://www.margaretthatcher.org/document/109439

17. Charles G. Hanson, *Taming the Trade Unions: A Guide to the Thatcher Government's Employment Reforms, 1980-90* (Basingstoke and London: Macmillan in association with the Adam Smith Institute, 1991), p. 15

18. Department of Employment, *Trade Union Immunities* (London: Her Majesty's Stationery Office, 1981), January 1981

19. Keith Joseph, *Solving the Union Problem Is the Key to Britain's Recovery* (London: Centre for Policy Studies, 1979), p. 6. See also Peter Dorey, "The Stepping Stones Programme: The Conservative Party's Struggle to Develop a Trade-Union Policy, 1975–79," *Historical Studies in Industrial Relations* 35 (2016); Paul Smith and Gary Morton, "The Conservative Governments' Reform of Employment Law, 1979-97: 'Stepping Stones' and the 'new right' agenda," *Historical Studies in Industrial Relations,* no. 12 (2001)

20. Charles G. Hanson, *Thatcherism, Trade Unionism and All That* (Adam Smith Institute); available from http://www.adamsmith.org/blog/politics-government/thatcherism-trade-unionism-and-all-that/

21. https://www.gov.uk/government/organisations/office-of-the-commissioner-for-protection-against-unlawful-industrial-action

22. See Huw Beynon, "False Hopes and Real Dilemmas: The Politics of the Collapse in British Manufacturing," *Critique: A Journal of Socialist Theory,* no. 16 (1983)

23. See Jean Hartley, John Kelly, and Nigel Nicholson, *Steel Strike: A Case Study in Industrial Relations* (London: Batsford, 1983)

24. See Orgreave Truth and Justice Campaign at https://otjc.org.uk/

25. DTI, *Industrial Action and Trade Unions* (London: Department of Trade and Industry, 1996), White Paper, cm 3470

26. Anthony Blair, "We Won't Look Back to the 1970s," *The Times*, 31 March 1997

27. The Major Government's 1993 *Trade Union Reform and Employment Rights Bill* abolished the 26 wages councils

28. William Brown, "Operation of the Low Pay Commission", *Employee Relations* 24, no.6 (2002) p. 497

29. Council Directive 94/45/EC

30. EU, 2002 Directive 2002/14/EC

31. A Court of Appeal ruling in July 2017 obliged employers to consult with unions on workplace issues – such as working hours and holiday pay – that affected members

32. Barbara Kersley et al., *Inside the Workplace: Findings of the 2004 Workplace Employment Relations Survey* (London and New York: Routledge, 2006)

33. See e.g. Peter A. Hall and David Soskice, *Varieties of Capitalism: The Institutional Foundations of Comparative Advantage* (Oxford University Press, 2001). Also Katherine Thelen, *Union of Parts, Labour Politics in Post-War Germany* (Ithaca, New York: Cornell University Press, 1991)

34. TUC, *Democracy in the Workplace: Strengthening Information and Consultation*, Economic Report Series (London: Trade Union Congress, 2014), p. 7

35. Ibid, p. 31

36. For an example of ICE arrangements in union avoidance see Alan Tuckman and Jeremé Snook, "Between Consultation and Collective Bargaining? The Changing Role of Non-Union Employee Representatives: A Case Study From the Finance Sector," *Industrial Relations Journal* 45, no. 1 (2014). For more on non-union employee arrangements see Gregor Gall, "Organizing Non-Union Workers As Trade Unionists in the 'New Economy' in Britain," *Economic and Industrial Democracy* 26, no. 1 (2005)

37. COUNCIL DIRECTIVE 93/104/EC of 23 November 1993 concerning certain aspects of the organization of working time, at http://eur-lex.europa.eu/legal-content/EN/TXT/PDF/?uri=CELEX:31993L0104&from=EN

38. DTI, *Fairness at Work* (London: Department of Trade and Industry, 1998)

39. Helge Hoel, Charlotte Rayner and Cary L. Cooper, *Workplace*

Bullying (London: John Wiley & Sons Ltd, 1999)

40. A terminology taken from Albert O. Hirschman, *Exit, Voice and Loyalty: Responses to Decline in Firms, Organizations and States* (Cambridge, Massachusetts and London, England: Harvard University Press, 1970).

41. Charles G. Hanson and Graham Mather, *Striking Out Strikes: Changing Employment Relations in the British Labour Market*, Hobart Papers (London: Institute of Economic Affairs, 1988)

42. Ministry of Justice, *Review of the Introduction of Fees in the Employment Tribunals* (London: Ministry of Justice, 2017), cm 9373

43. Ben Crawford, *Trade Unions Can Fix Our Employment Tribunal Disaster* (IER, 14February2017 2017); available from http://www.ier.org.uk/blog/trade-unions-can-fix-our-employment-tribunal-disaster

44. Ministry of Justice 2017, table 40, p. 99

45. PRESS SUMMARY R (on the application of UNISON) (Appellant) v Lord Chancellor (Respondent) [2017] UKSC 51 On appeal from: [2015] EWCA Civ 935, https://www.supremecourt.uk/cases/docs/uksc-2015-0233-press-summary.pdf

46. Brian Abbott, "The New Shop Stewards – the Citizens' Advice Bureaux?," *Employee Relations* 20.6 (1998)

47. *BIS, Trade Union Membership 2013: Statistical Bulletin* (London: Department for Business, Innovation and Skills, 2014). p. 5. See also BIS, *Trade Union Membership: Statistical Bulletin* (London: Department of Business, Innovation and Skills, May 2016)

48. BIS, ibid, 2016, p.16

49. TUC, *TUC Directory 2015* (London: Trade Union Congress, 2016)

50. TUC, *Only One in Every Forty New Jobs Since the Recession Is for a Full-Time Employee, Says TUC*, Available: http://www.tuc.org.uk/node/121494. Date Accessed: 15 November 20

51. Ibid, p. 12

52. Certification Officer, *Annual Report of the Certification Officer: 2013-14*. London: Certification Officer for Trade Unions and Employers' Associations, 2014

53. From figures submitted to the Certification Officer. The NUM, because of its federal structure, reports by Regional Organisation. This is based on the national and remaining regional/divisional figures

54. Ibid; 1980 figures from Jack Eaton and Colin Gill, *The Trade Union Directory: A Guide to All TUC Unions, Workers' Handbook* (London: Pluto Press, 1981)

55. TUC, *TUC Directory 2015*

56. See Maggie Craig, *When the Clyde Ran Red* (Edinburgh & London: Mainstream Publishing, 2011).

57. See *The Pop Up Union: A Postmortem* ·(http://www.solfed.org.uk/brighton/the-pop-up-union-a-postmortem,); available from https://libcom.org/library/pop-union-postmortem

58. The campaign formed the basis for the Ken Loach 2000 film, *Bread and Roses*

59. Jane Wills, *Mapping Low Pay in East London* (London: TELCO's Living Wage Campaign, 2001)

60. An interesting account of the recent IWW campaign in the UK by one of its activists

61. The relationship between the IWW, which is Glasgow based, and the London based IWGB is complex and based on a split in the summer of 2012. The basis of IWGB was the 'Cleaners and Facilities Branch', University of London outsourced workers. Members of UNISON at the time, they left en masse in April 2013 and then set up the University of London Branch of the IWGB

62. ONS, *Labour Disputes in the UK: 2015* (2 August 2016); available from https://www.ons.gov.uk/employmentandlabourmarket/peopleinwork/workplacedisputesandworkingconditions/articles/labourdisputes/2015#main-points

63. Ibid

64. H. A. Clegg, *The System of Industrial Relations in Great Britain* (Oxford: Basil Blackwell, 1972) p. 316

65. This can be found in autobiographical accounts of 'change maker' managers of the period, for instance the reminiscences of Michael Edwardes, *Back From the Brink: An Apocalyptic Experience* (London: Collins, 1983). The changes in management, challenging bureaucracy with flexibility and delegation, are most represented in the work of Tom Peters. Anecdotal evidence also points to the continuance, if at a reduced level, of short unreported stoppages and walk-outs

66. The words of Steve Baker Conservative MP for Wycombe, HC Official Report, 6 November 2013: Column 241 and onwards, cited in Bruce Carr QC, *The Carr Report: The Report of the Independent Review of the Law Governing Industrial Disputes: A Report From Bruce Carr QC to Government* (London: HMSO, 2014)

67. Ibid

68. See http://www.unitetheunion.org/growing-our-union/organising-toolbox/leverage

69. The Review cites photographs on RMT London Calling (23 April 2009) RMT Drivers Strike for Justice [online] Available: http://www.rmtlondoncalling.org.uk/node/509 as the evidence

70. https://carr-review.independent.gov.uk/wp-content/uploads/2014/04/2014-06-10-TUC-letter.pdf

Chapter 3
The Trade Union Act 2016:
A Guide

1. Introduction

Having abstained from any major tightening of control over trade unions and industrial action during the coalition government, the Conservative Party Manifesto for the 2015 election promised major 'reform'. Drawing on dusty proposals from the Major Government, and proposals from right wing organisations such as the Institute for Economic Affairs and the Taxpayers Alliance, they promised that an incoming Conservative government would introduce a range of draconian measures. They proposed: a tightened threshold in industrial action ballots, particularly in the public sector; to restrict the use of facilities time for trade union representatives; to restrict means for payment of trade union subscriptions; an increase in the powers of the Certification Officer in the regulation of trade unions; to extend what was to be considered intimidation against non-strikers; and to repeal regulations prohibiting the use of agency staff to replace strikers. When the proposals were published after the election, measures were added designed to restrict payment into trade union political funds, proposals which would seriously affect Labour Party funding. While these measures were to be presented as an attempt to modernise the law on trade unions, they were clearly retrograde and rooted deep in neoliberal thinking. Rather than modernisation, the measures were part of a dual process which, on the one side, was designed to tighten and contain trade union action – kettling the trade unions – on the other its intent was to return the trade unions to their status and position at the time of Taff Vale. The proposals not only aimed to restrict the immunities granted in the 1906 Trade Union Act, but also appears to reinforce a dramatic extension of the definition of intimidation by strikers. For example, where trade union officials were prosecuted for the use of the term 'blackleg' during the Taff Vale strike, now the shouting of 'scab' might be a criminal act.

The nature of the Bill, and its transition to the Trade Union Act 2016, is the subject of this section, following the Conservative's unexpected victory in the 2015 election and re-election in 2017. But first we might consider an unexpected twist: the Conservative government has attempted to present itself as 'a government for working people.' In part, this was justified by their eventual support for the National Minimum Wage (NMW), a total U-turn on their part since its introduction by the Labour government in 1998. They also started to voice support for a living wage, which campaigners argued for at a more realistic level for subsistence. In his first budget the Chancellor, George Osborne, announced a rather different 'new National Living Wage ... set ... to reach £9 an hour by 2020... compulsory ... (for working) people aged 25 and over.' The proposal fell short of the aspirations of the Living Wage campaign which, at the time of the budget announcement, was advocating a Living Wage of £9.40 in London and £8.25 elsewhere, based on the cost of living in 2016.[1] The fundamental position of the government, however, was the promotion of public spending cuts and 'austerity'. The National Living Wage (NLW) was clearly not an act of altruism by the government but linked to their policy of austerity, intended to shift the burden of support away from in-work benefits to wages paid by the employer with little, if any, net increase in income to the low paid. The manifesto made promises of cuts in welfare of £12 billion, although without specifying where this would come from – and something that the government had to quickly abandon. The introduction of the NLW can also be seen as an attempt to deflate growing militancy amongst some sections of the low paid, some of which had fueled the campaigns of the contract cleaners and cycle messengers.[2] The government's version of the NLW clearly presented problems for low paid workers. Firstly, it was limited to the over-25s so it did not apply to large sectors of low paid workers. Second, rather than an increase in pay, the NLW led to the imposition of new contracts for many workers, enforcing reductions to the minimum wage for overtime and unsocial hours, as well as loss of paid meal breaks and other squeezing of official working hours. Finally, the living wage is based on a full working week, of at least 36-hours,[3] and not on the precarious livelihoods experienced by increasing numbers of workers faced with uncertainty, especially of

Box 3.1:

Clause 1: The Act amends the Trade Union and Labour Relations (Consolidation) Act 1992. (Referred to here as TULR 1992)

zero-hours contracts. Within this there might be question as to where Conservatives – and their neoliberal ideologues – considered the legitimate role of trade unions to be. At least for skilled workers in the 19th century, while engaged in representation if not collective bargaining with employers, the trade union – formally designated a friendly society – provided sickness, unemployment and death benefits to members as well as strike pay. We might also speculate where this fits within a broader vision of the rolling back of the welfare state, to be replaced by individual provision of benefits.

Introducing the Bill in the House of Commons the Secretary of State for Business at the time, Sajid Javid, might have appeared to be proposing measures supporting trade unions. He explained to the Commons how unions 'have helped to secure higher wages, safer workplaces and stronger employee rights. They have fought for social justice and campaigned for freedom and democracy' and added, on a personal note how, '(unions) helped my father when he first worked in the cotton mills. They helped him again when a whites-only policy threatened to block him from becoming a bus driver.'

This, however, was a Bill intended as the final *coup de grâce* on an already weakened movement. Apart from the strikes around 'new unionism' of the low paid, the government's primary concern was with industrial action amongst public sector workers: strikes which had mobilised civil servants, teachers, and later junior doctors, all concerning changes in contract introduced by government. Some commentators of the right didn't think the Bill went far enough in terms of limiting the unions. Leo McKinstry in *The Spectator* argued that the government: 'should further consider ending the unions' immunity from claims for damages arising from strikes.'[4] Austerity policies, as well as continuing a cap on public sector pay, were likely to target public sector working conditions further, with wage increases falling well behind even the relatively low level of inflation experienced by the UK economy.

What was less expected was the vote in favour of leaving the European Union, which will mean that the rights of trade unions to organise and take industrial action under EU legislation are likely to be lost. Despite government claims to the contrary, many of the gains in employment protection emanate from EU Directives, such as on maternity rights, on employee voice, on transfer of undertakings, and – the particular bugbear of UK neoliberals – the working time directive, are possible targets in the 'bonfire of regulation' promised by the Conservatives. As 1980s trade union legislation had been passed to ease the transition to

Thatcherism and the neoliberalism that underpinned it, the 2016 *Trade Union Act* is designed to contain any militant reaction to its final accomplishment. The government's own estimates were that the balloting measures within the Bill would reduce strikes by 65%,[5] an assumption challenged by their own Regulatory Policy Committee.

Not only is the legislation designed to kettle the unions – to seriously restrict their action through legal constraint – it was also designed to undermine them economically, to effectively bankrupt them. Estimates of the immediate cost to the trade unions of measures required in the Bill totaled £11 million in familiarisation and training of officers and members, with further costs of £26 million over the next five years, with a considerable increase in postal and balloting costs.[6] However, the government's own assessment argued that they 'do not anticipate this measure imposing significant costs to trade unions or any other business or civil society organization.'[7] Suspicion that the intention was to attack union funds became more apparent as the debate on the Bill developed. The government justification for postal, rather than electronic, ballots for industrial action – particularly with the need to repeat these after six months – and despite their widespread use elsewhere could only have been because of the cost to unions rather than the claimed lack of security.

Opposition to the Bill came from human rights and trade union organisations. In a joint declaration, *Liberty*, the *British Institute of Human Rights* (BIHR), and *Amnesty International* UK argued that:

'By placing more legal hurdles in the way of unions organising strike action, the Trade Union Bill will undermine ordinary people's ability to organise together to protect their jobs, livelihoods and the quality of their working lives. ... We owe so many of our employment protections to Trade Unions and we join them in opposing this bill.'[8]

Criticism even came from the ranks of senior Conservative backbenchers: David Davis, a former shadow Home Secretary and later Minister responsible for the negotiation of a Brexit deal, compared some requirements of the Bill to Franco's Spain, in a widely reported interview on Sky News.[9] Lord Monks, previously General Secretary of the TUC, argued the Bill was 'an attack on civil liberties, flouting international standards and singling out unions for draconian intervention. It has little real support from employers, has been rushed through without proper consultation and should never have seen the light of day.'[10]

There was pressure from Scotland and Wales for the measures in the Bill to apply only to England and not across all the UK. Strong opposition came from the Scottish National Party (SNP) in the Commons, and the Welsh Assembly passed a resolution opposing the Bill and claiming that the measures fell within their remit and not of the Westminster Parliament.[11]

The campaign against the Bill was quickly mobilised. Before the election, Unite, Britain's largest union, changed its rule book deleting the words requiring that support is given 'so far as (action) may be lawful.' In an article in *The Guardian* Len McCluskey, Unite General Secretary, linked this move directly to the proposals in the Conservative Manifesto. 'It is no exaggeration' McCluskey argued 'to say that the right to strike in this, the first country of free trade unionism, was and is hanging by a thread. Should there be a Conservative majority in May, there will be a new attack on trade union rights and democracy.'[12] Dave Prentis, leader of Unison, the second largest UK union, also warned that 'nothing is ruled out' if the law on trade unions and industrial action is made more restrictive.[13]

By the end of July, two weeks after the publication of the Bill, a packed meeting of trade unionists and campaigners was held in Mander Hall at the National Union of Teachers head office in Central London addressed by a number of trade union leaders, including McCluskey and Prentis. John Hendy from the *Institute of Employment Rights* (IER) challenged the legality of the proposed measures in international law. The meeting was also addressed by John McDonnell who had proposed a *Trade Union Rights and Freedoms Bill* as a private members Bill in 2006.[14] McDonnell was at the time running Jeremy Corbyn's first campaign for leadership of the Labour Party after the 2015 election and the resignation of Ed Miliband. McDonnell promised that a future Labour government would replace the Conservative legislation set in place since 1980 and any further legislation that might be passed by the current government.[15] Not only was there a campaign mobilising to challenge the Trade Union Bill, with a strategy promoting both a legal and parliamentary challenge, but there were also calls to take to the streets in a series of demonstrations. The protest was also becoming linked to the growing campaign for Jeremy Corbyn to become leader of the Labour Party.

While it seemed that the Bill was to be railroaded through the political process it was not until the following May, and the last week of the Parliamentary session, that the somewhat amended *Trade Union Bill* completed the process to become an Act of Parliament. Each section –

on ballots, picketing, facilities time, political funds, and the role of the certification officer came under 'line-by-line scrutiny' in both the House of Commons Committee, where a range of witnesses gave evidence, and in the House of Lords.

The remainder of this section examines the different clauses of the Bill covering balloting, picketing, political funds, check-off, and the role of the certification officer. It examines some elements of the debate on the Bill, especially where measures were modified or even abandoned, and indicates the final form which received Royal Assent on 4th May 2016, although most of the *Trade Union Act 2016*, including the important ballot thresholds, came into effect in March 2017 and is yet to be tested.

2. Industrial Action Ballots

Ballot Thresholds

The proposals in the Bill which had the most initial coverage, described by the government Minister who steered it through the Commons as 'the flagship element,'[16] were the ballot thresholds proposed directly in the Conservative 2015 election manifesto. To be valid, an industrial action ballot required 'at least 50% of those who were entitled to vote'[17] to vote

Box 3.2:

Clause 2 & 3 Ballot thresholds for industrial action
Thresholds:
2. For industrial action postal ballots which require 'at least 50% of those who were entitled to vote in the ballot did so'.
3. Additionally, in important public services, 40% of those entitled to vote are required to vote in support of the action.
Important public services are defined in the Act as:
(a) health services;
(b) education of those aged under 17;
(c) fire services;
(d) transport services;
(e) decommissioning of nuclear installations and management of radioactive waste and spent fuel;
(f) border security.

in favour of the action. Further to this, in what were described as 'important public services' then 'at least 40% of those who were entitled to vote in the ballot answered 'Yes' to the question.'[18] The 'important public services' (see Box 3.2) were to be defined as those working in health services; the education of those aged under 17; fire services; transport services; decommissioning of nuclear installations and management of radioactive waste and spent fuel; and, border security. This further hurdle, it was proposed, was also to apply to those 'ancillary to the provision of important public services.' The measures were put out to a separate consultation,[19] one of three established for the Bill. Importantly, these thresholds applied to positive votes in favour, so that any failure to vote by anyone entitled to, or any abstentions, automatically counted alongside the votes against action (see Box 3.3). The government's own illustration of this point indicates that if 1000

Box 3.3: Threshold Requirements

Clause 2: Ballots: 50% turnout requirement
... where 1000 union members constitute the bargaining unit affected by the dispute, this clause means that at least 500 of those members would need to vote in order for the ballot to be valid. If 500 had voted, then a simple majority of them would need to vote in favour in order for the ballot to lead to industrial action: that would be 251 members. If all 1000 had voted, 501 would need to vote in favour.

Clause 3: Ballots: 40% support requirement in important public service
... where 1000 union members make up the bargaining unit affected by the dispute, as per Clause 2 the 50% participation threshold would need to be met: so at least 500 members would need to vote. The next test would be to determine whether the dispute was within an important public service and subject to the 40% threshold. If it was, then at least 40% of the 1000 members entitled to vote would need to vote in favour to enable industrial action. That means at least 400 members would need to vote in favour to enable action. A simple majority is still required in all ballots, so if all 1000 members had voted, then 501 votes in favour would be required to enable action.

Trade Union Bill: Explanatory Notes (House of Commons, 15 July 2015)

---

trade union members are balloted for industrial action then it would require more than 50%, that is at least 501 to vote in favour. However, if this is in the 'important public services' the action would require that an absolute minimum of 40% of all members to be in favour. This figure remains the same even if the turnout is as low as 50%. So if only 500 members out of 1000 voted then it would not require 251 votes in favour but the 401, which is more than 80% voting in favour.

The government presented a far higher threshold for industrial action ballots than had put them into office. It was widely pointed out that the slim majority of 12 MPs was gained on the basis of 36.9% of the vote on a 66.1% turnout. Less than a quarter of the electorate voted for them. The Conservative government, and few of their MPs, including Sajid Javid the Secretary of State responsible for the initial introduction of the measure, would not have won based on the thresholds they were introducing for industrial action ballots. Perhaps ironically, it was the unelected chamber, the House of Lords, which rallied to the defense of democratic rights, although it fell short of attacking the government mandate.

The purpose of the ballot thresholds in the Trade Union Bill were clearly to reduce the number of strikes. The government argued that the measure would cut the number of strikes by 65%, an assumption which was questioned by their own Regulatory Policy assessment.[20] Research by Darlington and Dobson, published just after the introduction of the Bill, examined industrial action ballots carried out between 1997 and 2015 and concluded that evidence showed that 'unions have generally been overwhelmingly successful in winning majority 'yes' votes in favour of strike action under the existing legislation, it also provides evidence to suggest they have often failed to achieve the Tories' proposed 50 per cent participation threshold.'[21] More specifically, 85 of the 158 ballots they examined reached the 50%, however this tended to be in smaller strikes 'while 444,000 workers could have taken strike action because they had a turnout rate of over 50 per cent, 3.3 million workers would have been prevented from going on strike.' Forty per cent of the ballots in 'important public services' fell below the requirement for 40% voting in favour. Strikes in education were often presented as those the government were keenest to stop. Here, Darlington and Dobson argue only 19 of the 29 strike ballots would have been able to go ahead. While every ballot carried out at individual schools passed the 40% threshold, only two national strikes achieved this.

The creation of the category of 'important public services' was the subject of consultation, highly structured in the responses it solicited. The consultation asked respondents whether they considered these services to include: protection against loss of life/serious injury; maintenance of public safety and national security; enabling economic activity across a significant area of the economy; and enabling significant numbers of people to get to their place of work. While the earlier categories cover what conventionally might be excluded on purely public safety grounds, it is the challenge to economic activity that is clearly stressed in the consultation.[22] Was the public sector to be defined narrowly, to those directly employed by the state or its direct agencies, or – particularly important in the age of privatisation and the contracting out of services – applicable to those organisations and agencies in receipt of public money through contacts to perform some service within local or national government or the NHS? It is clearly the cost and inconvenience created by these strikes and not the immediate risk that concerns the government. They were attacking what the historian E.P. Thompson identified as 'the servant problem'[23]: the creation of inconvenience because those who have normally provided an often unrecognised service have failed to perform their 'duty', thus creating disruption to the normal routine. As the consultation puts it:

'Strike action which closes schools can create significant inconvenience, and sometimes a financial burden, for parents who need to look after their child and are consequently unable to go to work. Others need to pay for additional childcare. There is also an economic burden and knock-on effects for business continuity planning for those workplaces whose staff cannot get to work. Some of these parents will work in other public services such as the police, health, fire and transport and there will be a knock-on effect on those services too. Children's education is also disrupted by school closures.'[24]

In this rationale, therefore, school teaching is measured purely in terms of its role as childminder for parents at work.

In its efforts to restrict industrial action, the government created a category of 'important public services' not recognized in any other country or responsible agency. Normally there may be exclusions from 'the right to strike' but this is where there is serious risk to life or imminent danger from a withdrawal of labour.

Following complaint from the TUC, the International Labour Office (ILO) recommended that 'the support of 40 per cent of all workers to carry out a strike would constitute an obstacle to the right of workers' organizations to carry out their activities without interference', and thus be in contravention of international rule and human rights. Further, while it is acceptable to limit action by some 'essential services in the strict sense of the term,' where there is risk of imminent danger to life from a withdrawal, they 'express concern that this restriction would also touch upon the entire primary and secondary education sector, as well as all transport services.'[25]

Despite opposition, and ILO concerns about the 40% threshold, these remained in the Bill. However, the only amendment to the thresholds following consultation was that ancillary workers are no longer included within the higher ballot threshold. So, in the final Trade Union Act, for example, while teachers proposing industrial action will require a 40% vote in favour, this will not apply to teaching assistants. Controversy on what constitutes 'important public services' remained, clarified by a statutory instrument by the Secretary of State who was required to submit to Parliament. With the exception of guidelines on who is included within the category 'decommissioning of nuclear installations and management of radioactive waste and spent fuel', these were published in early 2017 (see Appendix 1).[26]

The tight ballot thresholds might lead to an increase in vexatious use of injunctions by employers to stop industrial action. These certainly seem to open up increased possibilities of finding both groups of workers to reclassify as 'important public servants' within the moving boundaries between public and private sectors, with the growing web of contracting. Some guidelines (see Appendix 1), such as for transport workers, seem to include all workers – including those working in the private sector – while, in education, the private sector is excluded. The whole definition of 'public' has changed within these definitions in a pragmatic attempt to catch targeted groups of workers: rather than addressing 'public servants' they are targeting 'some public services in which strike action could have widespread and serious consequences for the public.'[27]

There is also, of course, the potential for arguing over figures for the number of individuals entitled to vote. This has often been the basis of employer's applications for injunctions to halt industrial action under the law governing ballots before 2015. One claim about the possible consequences of balloting thresholds is worth noting, coming, as it does, from an unlikely source. In his blog, Bruce Carr QC, the author of the review into leverage tactics used by trade unions in industrial action, one of the central pieces of evidence used by the government to justify the Bill, has argued that far from reducing the incidence there may be an increase.

'The irony of the present Bill is that if anything, it is likely to increase the use of leverage campaigns as unions seek to avoid what they see as the unfairness of a collection of measures which erode both the lawfulness and the impact of strike action as well as draining off substantial amounts of income through the changes to check off arrangements (at least in the public sector).'[28]

The further containment of lawful official trade union action, alongside further attacks on working conditions, terms of employment, and employment rights, without any safety valve of collective bargaining is likely to lead to an increase in spontaneous unofficial action as an immediate response to incidents. Such action would not have immunity, so it would be open to employers seeking injunctions from the court and liability for union officers if the action continues. In the case of such

Box 3.4:

TULR Clause 21: Effective repudiation of unofficial industrial action

21.(1) An act shall not be taken to have been authorised or endorsed by a trade union ... if it was repudiated by the executive, president or general secretary as soon as reasonably practicable after coming to the knowledge of any of them.

(2) Where an act is repudiated—

(a) written notice of the repudiation must be given to the committee or official in question, without delay, and

(b) the union must do its best to give individual written notice of the fact and date of repudiation, without delay—

(i) to every member of the union who the union has reason to believe is taking part, or might otherwise take part, in industrial action as a result of the act, and

(ii) to the employer of every such member.

(3) The notice given to members must contain the following statement—

'Your union has repudiated the call (or calls) for industrial action to which this notice relates and will give no support to unofficial industrial action taken in response to it (or them). If you are dismissed while taking unofficial industrial action, you will have no right to complain of unfair dismissal.'

unofficial action, the existing *Trade Union and Labour Relations Act* (1992) which the 2016 Act amends, allows union officers to avoid this liability through 'effective repudiation' in writing at the earliest opportunity (see Box 3.4). By formally distancing themselves from unofficial action, union officials and the union itself can avoid liability to any legal penalty arising from the dispute. However, this would not exempt potential injunction and prosecution of lay trade unionists – branch officials, shop stewards, workplace representatives or other members – deemed appropriate by a court for those involved in industrial action which happens without a ballot achieving the required thresholds. Such a prosecution could easily escalate any dispute, as happened under the *Industrial Relations Act* when London dockers were imprisoned. One thing the architects of the Bill were attempting to avoid, however, was the creation of further heroes – or as they saw it, martyrs – for the labour movement.

Electronic Balloting

According to existing legislation contained in the 1992 Act, industrial action ballots are required to be carried out by post, 'by the marking of a voting paper by the person voting,'[29] something that the government had no intention of changing. Trade Unions, while objecting completely to the Bill, seemed to feel that some version would become law. One reform that could be made that would ease at least some of the problems faced by trade unions would be a move from postal to electronic ballots when calling for industrial action. If, as the government kept claiming, the intention of their Bill was to modernise the system, then it might seem realistic to assume that some form of electronic voting in trade union ballots would be an obvious move. Rick Rickuss, General Secretary of the union Community, made the point that:

> 'people are not stupid; they do everything online these days. You can do all your banking, you can sign legal documents – you can do everything possible online. To suggest that you cannot vote in a ballot because it is not safe and secure undermines the whole principle of the debate. I think if we had a sensible debate about how ballots are conducted, we might make some serious progress.'[30]

However, in these particular circumstances, the government questioned the security of such ballots. Despite online ballots becoming increasingly common, the government insisted – citing possible fraud – that ballots for industrial action should remain by the return of a ballot paper through the post.

The government argument, that the use of electronic balloting was insecure, seemed odd given that the Conservative Party itself had recently used this very method to select their candidate for the London mayoral election. Their claim was based largely around the work of the Open Rights Group (ORG), a 'digital campaigning group' who argue that 'for all the benefits, technological developments have created new threats to our human rights. We raise awareness of these threats and challenge them through public campaigns, legal actions, policy interventions and tech projects.'[31] They are particularly concerned about the use of e-balloting and have monitored its use in a number of elections and pilot schemes. Because the workings of the e-election cannot be directly observed by voters and candidates, unlike paper ballots, they raise 'concern' regarding the suitability of e-voting and e-counting for statutory elections.'[32] It is important to note that the ORG came to this conclusion mainly based on problems around observers within hastily established pilot schemes for local and national elections, 'statutory elections,' and had not examined trade union ballots.

Unions argued that if the objective of the measure was to seek a clear democratic mandate in industrial action ballots from as large a turnout as possible, then e-balloting were more likely to achieve this than postal ballots. Len McCluskey, General Secretary of Unite, told the House of Commons Committee considering the Bill that:

> 'if (David Cameron the then Prime Minister) is genuine about wanting to increase the turnout, given that he has expressed his concerns about low turnout, which all of us have concerns about, then he should move towards, and get involved in a proper debate about, modern methods of balloting – the same balloting that the Conservative party has just elected their London mayoral candidate with – and most importantly, secure workplace balloting. All of that is feasible. The Electoral Reform Society has said that that is easily achievable with independent assessors.'[33]

The government claim was that these thresholds are intended to avoid industrial action being called on the basis of very small turnouts. An amendment by the opposition, supported by the TUC, would have allowed the use of electronic voting, but was rejected on grounds of 'safety and security.' Nick Boles, the Industry Department Minister who steered the Bill through most of its Commons stages, continually argued that there were different types of election, that industrial action ballots were 'statutory elections, which are important because the public has a deep interest in their result and it is quite right that we should hold them to a higher standard than we do others.'[34] While the government continually made this claim, drawing from the ORG conclusions concerning very different types of elections, the suspicion was clearly that the insistence on postal ballots was because they would be more costly to the unions. The TUC estimated that a postal ballot cost about £1 for every member in printing and postage costs. This would be for a ballot that might have to be repeated if the dispute out of which it arose wasn't resolved. The measure was clearly an attack on the funds of trade unions rather than a defense of democratic procedures.

The issue was fought through the Parliamentary process and the Government sustained a defeat in the House of Lords. An amendment, proposed by Lord Kerslake (previously the head of the Civil Service), proposed the introduction of an inquiry into the security of electronic voting with the intention of finally using these as an alternative to postal ballots. In proposing this Lord Kerslake hinted at the reasoning behind the government objection to changing the mode of the ballot. 'If we are to apply these high tests before industrial action can be taken,' he argued, 'then it is incumbent on us to provide trade unions with the best practical means available to achieve the full participation of their members' (see Box 3.5).

Box 3.5:

Clause 4: Provision for electronic balloting – review and piloting scheme
(1) The Secretary of State shall commission an independent review, the report of which shall be laid before each House of Parliament, on the delivery of secure methods of electronic balloting for the purpose of ballots held under section 226 of the 1992 Act (requirement of ballot before action by trade union).
(2) The use of pilot schemes shall be permitted to inform the design and implementation of electronic balloting before it is rolled out across union strike ballots.
(3) The Secretary of State must consider the report and publish and lay before each House of Parliament his or her response to it.

In a letter marked 'Official-Sensitive', Nick Boles had written to senior Conservative politicians voicing his concern that some of the 'benchmark' measures in the Bill might be lost if concessions were not given.

'It is clear that the thresholds provisions (the flagship element of the Bill) will be defeated if we do not make some move towards accepting the possibility of electronic (or e) -balloting. This is a key priority for trade unions and was a key Opposition theme in the Commons. We can expect the Bill to come under considerable pressure from this issue in the Lords, and it will likely gain considerable currency amongst Peers. The Government's handling of this could be crucial to avoid losing votes on our strike ballot thresholds clauses (as the unions consider that the thresholds will be easier to meet if balloting was electronic, rather than exclusively postal as is currently the case). We propose committing ... to establishing a review charged with looking into alternative methods of voting for all union ballots, including industrial action. The review would be tasked to seek evidence around legitimacy, safety, fairness and security of voting to ensure a system that is workable and accountable. I would not propose that we should also announce the period in which the review would report, although I expect us to come under pressure to do so.'[35]

To defend the 'flagship element', the government defeated the Lords amendment in the House of Commons, proposing its own amendment supporting an inquiry into balloting security. This was without any clear commitment that e-balloting would be introduced as a cheaper and more efficient way of conducting industrial action ballots.

In November 2016, following the EU referendum and the resignation of David Cameron, and with a new Secretary of State for the Department of Business, Energy, and Industrial Strategy, the review was announced. Chaired by Sir Ken Knight, former Chief Fire and Rescue Advisor for England, the review was to investigate issues including:

* risks of interception, impersonation, hacking, fraud or misleading or irregular practices associated with electronic balloting
* if systems can be safeguarded to reduce risk of intimidation of union members and protect anonymity of voters
* security and resilience of existing practices of balloting union members[36]

Box 3.6:

Clause 5: Information to be included on the voting paper for industrial action

• The voting paper must include a summary of the matter or matters in issue in the trade dispute to which the proposed industrial action relates.
• When the action in question is short of a strike the paper must indicate the type or types of action proposed and when the action is expected to take place.
• The voting paper must indicate the period or periods within which the industrial action or, as the case may be, each type of industrial action is expected to take place

Information requirements associated with industrial relations ballots

The original version of the Bill contained the requirement that in a ballot for industrial action:

> 'The voting paper must include a reasonably detailed indication of the matter or matters in issue in the trade dispute to which the proposed industrial action relates.'

This seemed to open a space for considerable challenge by employers. What was meant by 'reasonably detailed'? The view of the trade union is often very different to that of the employer on what is the ultimate cause of the breakdown in relations. What is for one side a complex dispute concerning the fundamentals of the employment contract, for example, can, for the other, be exclusively an issue of pay. The Bill was modified in the Lords, and accepted by the Commons, that the ballot paper include 'a summary of the matters at issue.'[37] However, while this might temper the demand it still remains open for potential challenge by an employer, or another party, to try to get an injunction to stop industrial action on the grounds of the interpretation of the dispute as presented on the ballot paper.

The Minister argued that there was limited information currently given on ballot papers. This ignored the usual practice for the ballot paper to be accompanied by detailed accounts of the grievances that have led to the threat of action, presented by the union in the mailing of materials related to the vote. Like several measures within the Bill, this has taken what was often best practice by trade unions and then put it under legislative scrutiny and control, allowing challenges of interpretation from employers, members, or possibly others with the intention of vexatious or vindictive challenges, thus hampering industrial action. All give added grounds for application to the courts for an injunction over the interpretation of the dispute, action likely to further sour already strained relations between management and workforce.

There are also requirements in the Act which stipulate that in proposing industrial action, a trade union must give indication on the ballot of 'the type or types of industrial action' and 'the period or periods within which the industrial action or, as the case may be, each type of industrial action is expected to take place.' The measure ignores the normal dynamics of collective bargaining where industrial action ballots often occur as a part of the bargaining, with the threat of industrial action itself breaking an established stalemate in negotiation. According to the 2014 figures, for example, there were 550 postal ballots which resulted in votes by workers in support of industrial action while there were only 155 recorded strikes.[38] This means that some movement in the bargaining position took place, leading to trade unions withdrawing strike threats. Such instances are far more common than strike action itself.

Given the increased complexity of the industrial action ballot, the information which has to be reported to union members and employers at the close of the ballot (see Box 3.7), and ultimately the annual reports of the Certification Officer, has also become far more detailed especially

Box 3.7:

Clause 6: All trade union members entitled to vote must be informed of:

- The turnout,
- The numbers voting yes,
- The numbers voting no,
- Number of spoilt or invalid papers,
- Whether the number of votes meets the 50% requirement.
- Where the ballot applies to 'important public services', if this constitutes the required 40% of members entitled to vote.

Box 3.8:

Clause 7: If industrial action has taken place following a ballot, the trade union is required in its annual return to the Certification Officer to indicate:
(a) the nature of the trade dispute to which the industrial action related;
(b) the nature of the industrial action;
(c) when the industrial action was taken.

when involving 'important public services'. A union is also required to add to their annual return to the Certification Officer details of any ballots during the year, as well as the details of any industrial action which took place (see Box 3.8).

It must be remembered that this comes from a government that argued for a reduction of bureaucracy and regulation: these measures clearly increase the burden on trade unions. While the results of any ballot is likely to be overseen by an independent body, such as the Electoral Reform Society under contract by a union, this will be at extra cost to the union. Also problematic is the additional detail that could be subject to an injunction to halt any resulting industrial action. While two unions have membership of over one million, and may be able to add the additional demands to the routine work of existing officers, more than 30 trade unions affiliated to the TUC have less than 30,000 members, with around five of these with around a hundred or less. Some small and newly established unions that are not affiliated to the TUC will also face problems with resources. The IWGB, for example, has been central in several important disputes, although it operates with a minimal staff.

Timing of and Duration of Industrial Action

The essence of the *Trade Union Bill* can be found in Clause 8 (see Box 3.9), dealing with the notice period given to employers of industrial action, and the point at which this notice period might be put by the employer. The Act extends the existing period of notice from 7 to 14 days with the action needing to take place within four weeks of the ballot. The period of a pause between ballot and action – a 'cooling-off' period – is long established, dating back to Barbara Castle's proposals of the late 1960s. The initial intention of the period was to challenge 'wildcat

Box 3.9:

Clause 8: Two weeks' notice to be given to employers of industrial action

Fourteen day's prior notice of action to be given to the employer by the union. This might be reduced to seven days in agreement between union and employer.

strikes' – spontaneous walkouts – by insisting on a period of negotiation to try to get the issues causing the stoppage to be resolved quickly and without escalation. The rationale within previous proposals and legislation was the promotion of collective bargaining in these circumstances, with the intention of avoiding industrial action. The purpose of extending the period of notice in the *Trade Union Bill* is clearly rather different: 'to ensure that the employer has more time to make contingency arrangements should strike action go ahead. This may enable resources in the economy to be used more efficiently.'[39] Measures extending the notice period, alongside changes in regulation on employing agency staff to replace strikers, seem designed to inflame the atmosphere of any industrial dispute, rather than bringing reconciliation and rebuilding trust. That is, the employer is given the opportunity not to reengage with existing employees and their trade union to resolve differences, for a turn or return to the bargaining table to resolve the differences that have led to such an impasse, but to use the period to make contingencies to maintain activity without the strikers. In the circumstances, this is particularly dangerous to a harmonious resolution of any dispute.

Latterly, the Minister, Nick Boles, argued that the pause was to allow a negotiated settlement, a shift since the manifesto and the consultation. This led one member of the Lords to consider that these measures 'will give employers an incentive to engage at the local car park rather than in positive negotiations to reach a mutual settlement.'[40] In a rather strange twist (see Clause 8, Box 3.9), the Act allows for the notice period to be reduced from 14 to 7 days when there is agreement between the union and employer. It is unclear where such a concession might be negotiated, where the parties are unable to negotiate over the substance of the matter but, like many aspects of the Act it awaits cases and examples to emerge.

Expiry of industrial action mandate

The Bill initially proposed that there should be a four month limit on industrial action ballots, that 'industrial action that is regarded as having the support of a ballot shall cease to be so regarded at the end of the period of four months beginning with the date of the ballot.'[41] The government argument has been that a number of strikes, principally by teachers and by London Underground workers, were based on mandates from 12 or more months previously. As Nick Boles put it:

> 'We simply want to ensure that industrial action is based on a current mandate on which union members have recently voted, and that those members are still working for the employer where the industrial action is proposed. It should not be a legacy mandate based on a vote undertaken many months or years previously. … certain recent strikes that caused great disruption to members of the public but were based on very old mandates. There were strikes by the National Union of Teachers in July and March 2014 that were based on mandates from June 2011 and September 2012. In October 2013, there were strikes based on a mandate from November 2011.'[42]

However, this seperates industrial action from the bitter and protracted disputes in which they are often rooted. Typically, an industrial dispute might lead to 'on-off' industrial action; conflicts rumble periodically, sometimes around a bargaining table – considering often quite fundamental changes to employment conditions and contracts – and sometimes moving to the picket line. The introduction of a limit on ballot

Box 3.10:

Clause 9: Expiry of mandate for industrial action

(1) Industrial action that is regarded as having the support of a ballot shall cease to be so regarded at the end of the period, beginning with the date of the ballot– of six months, or of such longer duration not exceeding nine months as is agreed between the union and the members' employer.
(… this measure is) … without prejudice to the possibility of the industrial action getting the support of a fresh ballot.

mandates does nothing to resolve these disagreements, but will more likely prompt more immediate industrial action. The most likely result of these time limits, however, would be for employers to try to ride out a four months' mandate period with the knowledge that the union will not just have to return to members but also pay for a further, costly, re-balloting.

In a minor defeat for the government, the mandate period was slightly extended from their initial intention. In Clause 9 (see Box 3.10), the limit was finally set at six months, or up to nine months if both union and employer agree, before the mandate for the industrial action ballot expires. The tunnel vision of the Bill, concerned with restricting union ability to stage action rather than resolving the underlying cause of dispute, is clear in the provision for limiting mandates on any industrial action ballot.

Picketing

Nowhere in the Bill is the underlying ideology, rooted firmly in neoliberalism, and the intent of the Cameron government more obvious than in the changes proposed to the law on picketing. Much of what the government suggested was not contained within the Bill itself but could be found in the documentation for the consultation on 'tackling intimidation of non-striking workers.' This allowed what appeared a climb-down, or mellowing of view, without impacting on the substance of the final Bill.

Having effectively outlawed 'closed shop' agreements in 1980s legislation, neoliberals appeared set on breaking what they consider the other main 'monopoly practice' of trade unions. This highlights the roots of the Bill in the ideology of neoliberalism and specifically the writings of the Institute of Economic Affairs (IEA). For them, as Lord Harris – one of the founders of the IEA – put it in 2005, the very 'abuse' of 'peaceful picketing' is the means 'by which these monopoly suppliers of labour routinely enforced strikes to support wage demands and closed shops.'[43] The need for the IEA and neoliberals generally is to break the trade unions and their collective strength. If we look at the policy prescription offered by the IEA in Charles Hanson's proposals for reform in 1991, from which the present Bill seems to have drawn directly, we find his suggestion of the transfer of regulation, in this case the number of pickets, 'from the *Code of Practice on Picketing* to the statute book.'[44] The picket has also been the target for the wrath of right wing politicians[45], concerned that large numbers of workers, in their very assembly, constitute intimidation. Codes of Practice, while they in themselves do not lay down the legally enforceable regulation can, and will, be taken into account in any court proceedings. The latest *Code of Practice of Picketing* reflects the threat that:

> 'Violence and disorder on the picket line is more likely to occur if there are excessive numbers of pickets. Wherever large numbers of people with strong feelings are involved there is a danger that the situation will get out of control, and that those concerned will run the risk of committing an offence, with consequent arrest and prosecution, or of committing a civil wrong which exposes them, or anyone organising them, to civil proceedings.'[46]

Clearly there has been violence on picket lines, usually when an attempt is being made to bring in non-striking workers, and it is often the police attempting to break the picket which sparks trouble.

While there is immunity to action concerning enticement to the breach of employment contract relating to the pickets in a trade dispute, it indicates that strikers have no inherent right to picket. There is no right to stop anyone, or any right to stop a vehicle, from crossing a picket line. Such action, the Code indicates, constitutes the offence of inciting the driver to break their contract of employment. That:

> '... the law imposes certain limits on how, where and for what purpose such picketing can be undertaken. These limits help ensure proper protection for those who may be affected by picketing - including those who wish to cross a picket line and go to work.'[47]

Activities listed in the code which might happen during a picket, and might be considered as criminal offences are: the use of threatening, abusive, or disorderly behavior; the use or threat of violence; obstruction; possession of an offensive weapon; damaging property; breach of the peace; obstructing a police officer in the execution of his or her duty.[48] The particular danger here is that the very definition of what might constitute some of these – what, for example, is threatening or abusive – is subjective and being considered initially by police, and then by the courts, in circumstances that are already tense. For neoliberals the very existence of a picket line is considered an intimidation. While, as we have seen, the claims of intimidation in the Carr Review were at best tenuous, these same claims were recycled in the consultation.

It was initially suggested that a condition of industrial action would be that the trade union(s) involved would be required to produce a 'picketing and protest plan,' submitted to the local police. In this the union would need to specify when it was to hold protests or pickets associated with the action, where these were to be, and how many people would be involved. The consultation specifically points to the requirement that such a plan would have to contain information on:

- Whether there will be loudspeakers, props, banners etc.
- Whether it will be using social media, specifically Facebook, Twitter, blogs, setting up websites and what those blogs and websites will set out.[49]

The government argued that there was a 'growing use of social media as a modern tool which enables striking workers to show their feelings towards their non-striking colleagues.' Certainly this had been a CBI concern; that the law had not kept up with developments in technology.[50] There seemed to be two particular and distinct concerns with such a use of social media, one of which was more extensively discussed. Firstly, there were claims about the use of social media to intimidate both non-striking workers as well as management and employers; for example, by posting pictures. Secondly, and more implicitly, there are clear concerns that social media is being used to mobilise protests and pickets. However, and perhaps largely because of opposition from the police, these particular measures were not directly addressed in the final Act. In evidence to the House of Commons Committee on the Bill the police offered evidence which effectively countered the view of pickets being inherently violent. Deputy Chief Constable Hall, representing the Police Chiefs Council, argued that 'in the majority of cases, there is no real need for the police to be involved with industrial disputes and picketing. Indeed, our stance is that we would wish to avoid it if we can. Many pickets and industrial disputes run without any contact or involvement with policing.' Any incidents which did occur were clearly covered by existing legislation. 'On social media,' he argued:

> 'I do not believe that there is a need for the police to be able to vet or censor social media posts. Clearly, there may be a role for policing at some point. If things are posted that commit criminal offences, we would investigate in the same way that we would investigate other social media posts.'[51]

Ultimately no measures were introduced in the Act but with the warning that there will be a revision of the Picketing Code of Practice. When the Code did appear in 2017, there was no mention of social media or other technology.

However, subsequent to the passing of the Act there has been at least one example where the Act has seemed to be used to monitor a picket's use of their mobile phone. An organiser for the RMT union, during a 24-hour strike by Northern Rail workers, was ordered to hand over his mobile phone to his employer.[52] It is far from clear that this was based on any part of the actual *Trade Union Act 2016* or the Code of Practice which nowhere, in themselves, seem to legitimate such a scrutiny of

---

Box 3.11

Clause 10. Union supervision of pickets

The union is required to appoint a 'picket supervisor', who is an officer or member of the union, and who is familiar with the Code of Practice for Picketing issued by Acas (which is to be revised following the passing of the Act)

'The union or picket supervisor must take reasonable steps to tell the police—
(a) the picket supervisor's name;
(b) where the picketing will be taking place;
(c) how to contact the picket supervisor.
'The union must provide the picket supervisor with a letter stating that the picketing is approved by the union.'
'If an individual who is, or is acting on behalf of, the employer asks the picket supervisor for sight of the approval letter, the picket supervisor must show it to that individual as soon as reasonably practicable.'
'While the picketing is taking place, the picket supervisor must—
be present where it is taking place, or
be readily contactable by the union and the police, and able to attend at short notice.
'While present where the picketing is taking place, the picket supervisor must wear something that readily identifies the picket supervisor as such.'

---

communications. The passing of the Act might, however, have emboldened employers and the police in a more draconian implementation of existing legislation.

The consultation makes plain the general powers that were already available to police in criminalising potential activities of pickets through existing community orders:

'A Community Protection Notice (CPN) can be issued by a police officer or a local authority officer against any individual who is acting in a way that is having a detrimental effect on the quality of life of those in the locality, if the behaviour is persistent and unreasonable. A CPN can include restrictions on the individual's behaviour and breach of the terms of a Notice is a criminal offence and can result in a prison sentence. Where a number of complaints are made but nothing is seemingly done, an individual or business can activate the new community trigger. Each local area is required to set a threshold (for instance, three reports of anti-social behaviour in a six-month period or five separate reports about the same incident). When this threshold is met, local agencies will meet and agree next steps on possible action.'[53]

An important change introduced by the Act (Clause 10, see Box 3.11) is the requirement for the union to appoint a 'picket supervisor' responsible for each picket line established during a strike. This, the government argue, was incorporating advice that such a supervisor should be appointed from earlier codes, making it an obligation. This also criminalises contravention and encourages police intervention, making the union potentially subject to a court injunction and liable for compensation if even a minor breach takes place. The requirement to give their name to the police, any representative of the employer, and – in the original proposal – anyone who asked for it, left the supervisor vulnerable to blacklisting and potential retribution. What caused David Davis' much publicised comparison with measures by Fascist Spain and Nazi Germany[54] was the requirement for picket supervisors to wear a badge or armband to mark them out. All commentators, including the police in evidence to the Committee on the Bill,[55] have argued that the current code of practice has not created any problems and that if any trouble arises on a picket line, there are already adequate legal sanctions. Hence there was no real need to change current practice in this area.

There were some concessions to the original Bill but they were very limited. The Act no longer requires that a letter of authorisation should be presented to anyone who asks, which would have been a blatant invitation to blacklisting, but potential problems for any picket supervisor remain. As Keith Ewing has pointed out, while the picket supervisor is engaged in perfectly legal activity, if for some reason they refuse the request from a police officer to show the letter, then the picket might then be rendered illegal and be actionable by the employer. There is no requirement that the police need any reason for asking to see the authorisation, nor even that they are in uniform or provide their own authorisation or documentary evidence that they are police officers. The union is still required to inform the police of plans for any pickets or protests that might occur as part of the dispute. Picket supervisors are still required to have a letter of authorisation from the union which they need to show to police or a representative of the employer. While no longer required to wear an armband, picket supervisors are still required to wear something which identifies them.

Use of agency workers during strikes

One measure in the Conservative Party election manifesto which seemed designed to heighten tensions on some picket lines, if not promote a violent response, was the promise to 'repeal nonsensical restrictions banning employers from hiring agency staff to provide essential cover during strikes'. This meant the reform of Paragraph 7 of the *Conduct of Employment Agencies and Employment Business Regulations 2003*[56] to remove the stipulation that 'an employment business shall not introduce or supply a work-seeker to a hirer to perform … the duties normally performed by a worker who is taking part in a strike or other industrial action.' The repeal of the regulation is presented as a means of substantially ameliorating the impact of strikes.

The government estimated, with limited availability of replacement staff and the large number of strikes which involve a large number of workers on one day, that 'between 17% and 27% of working days lost due to industrial action will potentially be covered by temporary agency workers'. Notwithstanding the government's own Regulatory Policy Committee thinking that these figures lack any supporting evidence, there is a significant chance of the use of strikebreaking agency staff escalating tensions in any dispute. The trade body, the Association of Professional Staffing Companies (APSCo), argue that the main affected area would be education. The moving of the provision of supply teachers to private agencies, rather than local authority registers, means a potential strikebreaking workforce although, according to the APSCo, feedback in the sector suggests they think they will not be adversely affected due to supply teachers' reluctance to cross picket lines.

The views of the established recruitment professionals seem, at best, ambivalent to the change in regulation which would allow them to supply scab labour. Kate Shoesmith, Recruitment & Employment Confederation (REC) head of policy, said that: 'We are not convinced that putting agencies and temporary workers into the middle of difficult industrial relations situations is a good idea for agencies, workers or their clients.'[57] However, the danger is that not only will some of the established agencies move to taking on such contracts, new agencies will enter the market specifically to supply strikebreakers. While this might be limited in the case of skilled labour, with such targeted union actions amongst teachers and railway workers, it may become embedded against campaigns of low paid workers. A number of recent strikes have occurred amongst cleaners, couriers, and warehouse workers – often concerning the living wage – who themselves were employed through employment agencies. Even more dangerous would be the recruitment of this scab labour with the threat that turning down such work could lead to benefit sanctions. The worst aspect of the proposal is that it makes explicit any government enthusiasm to encourage the use of blackleg or scab labour during strikes, at the same time as potentially outlawing the use of these terms as intimidation.

The proposal itself was never a part of the Trade Union Bill but required a separate change of Regulation by the Secretary of State. When the Act came into force in March 2017, the Regulations had been revised – removing or modifying some regulations contained – but without any change to regulation 7, the prohibition on employment businesses providing scab labour. As the REC noted:

> On 4th May 2016, the Trade Union Bill received Royal Assent. The proposal to remove Regulation 7 is however subject to secondary legislation and so was not mentioned in what is now the Trade Union Act. We have been advised that the next steps for Reg 7 are still under consideration by government and we will keep members informed.[58]

This might not be laxness but due to a fundamental error in the proposal which does not distinguish the difference between 'employment businesses' and 'business agencies' as laid down in these very regulations. The key distinction is that workers placed by an agency remain employed by the agency while those placed by an employment business become employees of the client organisation. Within the existing regulations employment agencies can supply temporary workers during strikes. Employment agencies can, within existing regulations, supply temporary workers during strikes.[59] Employers currently can, and sometimes do, bring in temporary agency staff during a strike. Most strikes are short, mostly one or two days, the replacement of this temporary loss with permanent staff, while consistent with neoliberal freedom, would be limited only to the most provocative employer.

3. Political Funds

The Nature of Trade Union Political Funds

The most anti-democratic section of the Bill deals with the levying and use of political funds. This is especially clear when considered alongside measures to change constituency boundaries and change voter registration which are means to ensure a built-in Conservative majority within the voting system. It is certainly the clause which presents the greatest challenge to political representation and it received particular scrutiny in the House of Lords. The relationship between trade unions and politics has always been contentious. The roots lay in the very role and nature of trade unions within society where, as an organised voice in the interest of working people, they have always been an inherent threat to capitalist society. Some general and industrial unions, at their founding, had a broad aspiration to bring about a revolutionary transformation of the very nature of wage labour in capitalist society, through direct action rather than establishing a compromise with employers. Ultimately, either in principal or pragmatically, some compromise is reached between unions and employers which values collective bargaining rather than direct action. In the UK this gelled in a social democratic compromise, the establishment of the Labour Party as a vehicle for change, which – in part to suppress any syndicalist tendencies – gained primacy within the left of British politics. The trade unions, as economic agents of the working class, concerned with pay and conditions of employment, were separate from the Labour Party, which acted as its political wing seeking Parliamentary representation and broader political changes. The problem remained that the Party was established by the unions to further their class interests in Parliament, with the unions as the main source of funding for the Party.

Since the *Trade Union Act of 1913* the unions have been required to establish a political fund. In measures introduced in 1927, largely a vengeful response to the General Strike, union members were required to to opt-into payment to the funds. This measure was repealed by the post-war Labour government. However, this political funding, and the very relationship between trade unions and the Labour Party has remained contentious, and a weathervane for social democratic politics in the UK.

Under Thatcher, the rules on political funds were tightened; unions were required to ballot their membership if they wanted to establish a fund. Even when there was a majority in favour of a fund, members were allowed to opt-out of paying into the political levy. Unions were required to repeat these ballots every ten years. Thatcher and her government argued that, with a sizable minority of trade union members voting Conservative, they were being held hostage to the Labour Party by a left-wing leadership. However, this was soon found to be in error, as Charles Hanson – an IEA writer on trade union legislation – has commented, 'presumably the government expected that in some unions at least the vote would go against the continuation of the political fund. But if so, this particular piece of legislation seriously backfired, so that it ended up by encouraging rather than discouraging political funds which are frequently used to support the Labour Party in its political activities.'[60] Trade union members, when asked to establish a political fund, voted overwhelmingly to establish them and to renew them when the law required it.

Following complaints about an advertising campaign by NALGO (now part of Unison following a merger) the courts ruled that, despite no mention of a political party or prescriptions to vote or not vote, the challenge to government policy meant such expenditure should have come from political rather than the general fund of the union. In the 1984 Act the definition of political activity was extended to 'the production, publication or distribution of any literature, document, film, sound recording or advertisement the main purpose of which is to persuade people to vote for a political party or candidate or to persuade them not to vote for a party or candidate.' It became clear that, even when there was no subscription or affiliation to the Labour Party, if a union was to engage in any campaigning activity which might in any way be construed as questioning or challenging government policy, or even that of any political party, then a union needed to establish a separate political fund. Thirty eight unions carried out ballots following the 1984 legislation, with around 84% of members voting in favour. Not all those unions establishing political funds were affiliated to the Labour Party. Following the 1984 legislation, twenty non-affiliated unions successfully carried out ballots to establish political funds as an 'insurance policy' to protect their ability to campaign.[61] In the most recent report, the Certification Officer indicates that twenty-four unions currently have a political fund, the reduction since 1984 accounted for by union mergers. Of the three unions required to renew their fund in the last year, each achieved more than a ninety per-cent vote in favour.[62]

Reform of the Political Funds

A central proposal in the *Trade Union Bill 2016* was to shift members from being required to opt-in to payment to the political fund, rather than opting-out. This is despite the ease with which members can contract-out from payments under already existing law. Such a change, if it was implemented, would limit the funds to the Labour Party, restrict trade union campaigning, and as was raised in the debate on the Bill, limit support for other campaigning organisations which might be supported by individual trade unions.

Fourteen unions are affiliated to the Labour Party. In 2014 these affiliated unions raised £22 million in political funds, with about £10 million given to the party in affiliation fees and donations. The Labour Party received over £6 million a year from the trade unions, its major contributor.[63] Changes to the rules for political funds would lead to an estimated loss to the Labour Party of at least £1 million a year, although it could be far more. The justification the government gave for the changes was one of transparency despite it being pointed out in debate that all such payments were already in the public sphere. They also

Box 3.12

Clause 11. Political Funds

'It is unlawful to require a member of a trade union to make a contribution to the political fund of a trade union if—
(a) the member has not given to the union notice of the member's willingness to contribute to that fund (an 'opt-in notice'); or
(b) an opt-in notice given by the member has been withdrawn ...'

Box 3.13

Para 12: Union annual return to Certification Officer on Political Fund

The union annual return to the Certification Officer is required to detail expenditure from the Political Fund, when expenditure in any year exceeds £2,000 (an amount which may be changed by the Secretary of State and subject to Parliament). Payments from the Political Fund include contribution to the funds of, or providing property or services to, a political party; maintenance of a political office; holding, or attending where expenses are paid, a conference or meeting dealing with the business of a political party; or production of promotional material for a political party (from TULR Act 1992).

The report must give the name and amount to each political party, or candidate, donated to from the Political Fund.

It must also detail all other campaigns supported from the Political Fund, the report to the Certification Officer must detail:

"(a) the nature of each cause or campaign for which money was expended, and the total amount expended in relation to each one;
"(b) the name of each organisation to which money was paid (otherwise than for a particular cause or campaign), and the total amount paid to each one;
"(c) the total amount of all other money expended."

claimed that such a reporting obligation applied to employers' associations, although no associations contributed to a political party. Any of their member organisations, however, were free to make donations without any notification.

The figures indicate that while a sizeable proportion of money from union political funds is directed to the Labour Party, it is clear that most of it is used in campaigning. Many unions have now established a political fund specifically for campaigning. This campaigning, while seen to support the interests of union members, might clearly be seen as challenging government policy, especially since the government is the direct or indirect employer of the majority of trade union members. One of these unions, the Society of Radiographers, while not affiliated to the Labour Party, argued the efficacy of a political fund in support of the professional activity of their members to the House of Commons Committee on the Bill:

'Establishing a fund will ensure we continue to speak up on behalf of members, their patients and on behalf of the profession. Without a political fund we are concerned that we could be stopped from doing this by politicians who do not like what we say. When we speak out on issues such as hospital closures, patient safety, developing the role of the radiographer to allow prescribing and reporting, the impact of being a shortage profession in radiotherapy and against cuts in protected study time, we do so because our members want us to. We need to establish a political fund to ensure we can continue to do this, as is our democratic right, on behalf of members and their patients.'[64]

Following scrutiny in the House of Lords, and considerable controversy about long-standing cross party agreement on party funding arrangements, the proposal on trade union political funds was watered down but not abandoned. The Lords committee also fell back on the justification that such a measure had been included as an election promise by the Cameron government. Finally, the Bill was amended to allow a 12-month transition period for the new political fund arrangements and that only new trade union members would be required to opt-in (see Box 3.14).

The Bill specified that if the total political expenditure is greater than

Box 3.14

Para 11.5: Opting-in of new trade union members

only after the end of the [12 month] transition period, and only to a person—
(a) who after the end of that period joins a trade union that has a political fund, or
(b) who is a member of a trade union that has a political fund but did not have one immediately before the end of that period.

£2,000 then all details of this need to be itemised in the annual return to the Certification Officer. Such a move is likely to add to the controversy over trade union affiliations and the use of trade union funds. It is open to challenge by union members or any other party. The Labour Party was not the only beneficiary of union political funds. Unions maintain a political fund, used for general campaigning around relevant causes, usually originating in the outcome of conference decisions. In the Parliamentary debate, some of these organisations and causes supported by individual unions were cited, such as that given to the anti-racism organisation *Hope not Hate.* As well as support for political parties, political candidates, political promotion through media and publication, the unions are now required to detail for each supported organisation (see Box 3.14). Trade union support for such campaigns as the plight of the Palestinians has caused considerable controversy in the past, and is now potentially open to legal challenge despite support by a majority in union conferences.

4. Facilities Time and Check-off

Facilities Time

Under established legislation, employee representatives from recognised trade unions are entitled to time, often referred to as facilities time, to carry out activities covered by collective bargaining, representing members involved in discipline and grievance procedures, and to perform other duties associated with their union role (see Appendix 2 for list of duties). The Bill proposed substantial scrutiny of trade union facilities time used by representatives employed within the public sector. Under the new proposals, the Minister can ask any public authority: how many of their employees are union officers; how much was paid to them to cover facilities time for union duties; percentage of the overall wage bill that this represented; duties or activities being paid for as facilities time; provision of other facilities for union officers from the public authority employer. Armed with this data, the Minister has the power to 'make provision restricting rights of relevant union officials to facility time.'[65] This proposal posed potential restrictions on the activities of a range of representatives, some currently with statutory rights to time for union duties. For example, health and safety representatives and representatives involved in consultation over redundancy, as well as learning and equality representatives and branch officers engaged in day-to-day representation of members, general consultation with employers, and a whole range of issues which might be subject to collective bargaining would be open to intense scrutiny.

The assault on facilities time followed a campaign by the Taxpayers Alliance, which claimed that the payment for trade union duties within the public sector was costing taxpayers at least £85 million a year. A major failing of the Taxpayers Alliance's approach was that they considered only the cost and not the benefit of such representation. The role of workplace representatives is well documented. Research from the University of Leeds, jointly published by the Department of Business, Innovation and Skills, TUC and CBI talked of the 'mutual benefits' of the valuable work being done by these representatives.[66] Acas has produced a Code of Practice which details the duties and activities that trade union officers perform (see Appendix 2). It is not surprising that a government consultation regarding the facilities being offered to the approximately 200,000 workplace representatives in the UK indicated that the representatives were hard working and under considerable pressure:

'... some of those representatives face problems in successfully balancing their normal work duties with their representative functions. This situation can place excessive pressure on them, and can lead to their under-performance as workplace representatives. The Government believes that as a consequence the benefits which representatives can bring to the workplace are not being fully realised.'[67]

While many had voiced their criticism of the 40 per-cent threshold on 'important public sector' ballots, a large number of local authorities voiced opposition to the measures on facilities time. All pointed to the valuable role that trade union officers had played, especially at turbulent times. The Leader of Ealing Council is typical in arguing that:

'the reasonable provision of facility time for trade union officers is an important part of ensuring the effective operation of the workplace in a collective bargaining environment. While ensuring that facility time remains proportionate and justifiable is a sensible aim, within local government at least this is largely achieved under the current system. The requirement to record and publish details of facility time would be an administrative burden on stretched local authority budgets. Further, any centrally imposed cap on facility time, as the bill enables, would run the risk of being too inflexible to cope effectively with periods when higher levels of facility time are required, such as when a part of the council is undergoing significant change or re-organisation.'[68]

Of course, this does beg the question as to whether the framers of the Bill sought, or sought to undermine, a 'collective bargaining environment.' Most evidence from the local authorities, as well as from the Scottish Parliament and the Welsh Assembly, spoke of how they had cultivated a partnership with the unions representing their workforce, which had proved both amicable and productive. In evidence to the House of Commons Committee, the Directorate of NHS Wales argued that:

'In general, partnership working between employer organisations and trade unions works well in NHS Wales and we have established effective working relationships which support the development of effective and mutually beneficial solutions to a number of significant challenges which the service has addressed and continues to face. It is our view that the NHS's workforce challenges are best addressed by an efficient, engaged and productive workforce, where there is regular consultation and ongoing dialogue with our staff and a key element of this approach is through social partnership with trade unions representing NHS staff.'[69]

Box 3.15

Para 13.3: Information requirements on Facilities Time

(3) The information that is within this subsection is information relating to facility time for relevant union officials including, in particular—

(a) how many of an employer's employees are relevant union officials, or relevant union officials within specified categories;

(b) the total amount spent by an employer in a specified period on paying relevant union officials for facility time, or for specified categories of facility time;

(c) the percentage of an employer's total pay bill for a specified period spent on paying relevant union officials for facility time, or for specified categories of facility time;

(d) the percentage of the aggregate amount of facility time taken by an employer's relevant union officials in a specified period that was attributable to specified categories of duties or activities;

(e) information relating to facilities provided by an employer for use by relevant union officials in connection with facility time.

While the Taxpayers Alliance had estimated that the cost of facilities time was approximately £85 million per annum, others estimated the benefit. In an examination of a range of research carried out for the TUC, Gregor Gall drew on the following estimates from work in 2004:

- Dismissal rates were lower in unionised workplaces with union reps – this resulted in savings related to recruitment costs of £107–£213m pa.
- Voluntary exit rates were lower in unionised workplaces with union reps, which again resulted in savings related to recruitment costs of £72–£143m pa.
- Employment tribunal cases were lower in unionised workplaces with union reps resulting in savings to government of £22–£43m pa.
- Workplace-related injuries were lower in unionised workplace with union reps resulting in savings to employers of £126–£371m pa.
- Workplace-related illnesses were lower in unionised workplace with union reps resulting in savings to employers of £45–£207m pa.[70]

Updating these estimates for 2014 shows an overall benefit of £476 – £1,250 million pa. The public-sector proportion of this is 58% – giving a crude public-sector benefit of £276 – £725 million pa saving.

The Bill was ultimately amended, not to scrap the proposals on monitoring the duties of employee representatives but to allow for a period of three years grace, with the collection of three years' worth of data on facilities time by the public authority, before the Minister can exercise reserve powers to limit facilities time. This will allow the Minister responsible to scrutinise future data on union duties and isolate authorities and departments where this is considered excessive. However, as many of the employer witnesses to the Parliamentary committee stage of the Bill argued, in periods when the time spent on union duties was particularly high, this was – counter to the Taxpayer Alliance argument – because representatives were attempting to resolve important issues in partnership with management. In the circumstances, the cost of the collection of the required data on the time given to employee representatives to perform their duties might be far higher than any savings made.

Check-off

Trade union dues might originally have been collected by a workplace representative, the shop steward, who could use this collection round as an opportunity to talk to members about any problems and give feedback on any issues. This, of course, not only required the existence of a trade union representative but also that they had adequate time for a regular round of members. Many collective agreements in both the public and private sector include the possibility of union subscriptions being paid by deduction from pay, as 'check-off'. Thatcher-era legislation put limits on this, requiring the worker to renew permission for check-off every three years. Employers usually made some small charge for the cost of this deduction. Many unions have increasingly moved to payment of regular subscription through a direct debit from the member although check-off remains particularly important for many low-paid workers. While not in the original Bill, an amendment was added in committee to end check-off. This was, then, not a manifesto promise but the continuation and extension of an ongoing campaign of attrition against civil service unions already in play by the Conservatives during the

---

Box 3.16

Para 14.2 Reserve Powers of the Minister

The reserve powers may not be exercised so as to apply to any particular employer unless—
(a) a Minister of the Crown has given notice in writing to the employer—
(i) setting out the Minister's concerns about the amount of facility time in the employer's case, and
(ii) informing the employer that the Minister is considering exercising the reserve powers in relation to that employer;
(b) the employer has had a reasonable opportunity to respond to the notice under paragraph (a) and to take any action that may be appropriate in view of the concerns set out in it; and the powers may not be exercised until after the end of the period of 12 months beginning with the day on which the notice under paragraph (a) was given.

---

period of the Coalition Government, drawing on the Taxpayers Alliance. The Public and Commercial Services union (PCS) had already seen moves by the Home Office, the Department for Work and Pensions (DWP), and by HM Revenue and Customs to drop 'check-off.' This was clear evidence of an attack on union funding, an attempt to curb a union which had challenged government attempts at undermining conditions of service within the civil service. Unions became increasingly concerned that this would lead to a loss of membership as low paid workers drop membership rather than switch to payment by direct debit.[71]

Following earlier publication of the Bill, the government announced that it would introduce an amendment 'to abolish the practice of 'check-off' across all public-sector organisations, modernising the relationship between employees and trade unions.'[72] Like their arguments for the rest of the Bill, this was presented as an opportunity to 'modernise' industrial relations. Rather than the dated system of deduction by the employer when 'people didn't have bank accounts', this would release the employer from an administrative and financial burden involved in collecting these union subscriptions. Matt Hancock, Cabinet Office Minister, announcing the amendment to the Bill argued that '(i)n the 21st century era of direct debits and digital payments, public resources should not be used to support the collection of trade union subscriptions.'

Check-off was the result of existing collective agreements between civil service departments and the recognised trade unions and, of course, the government's moves were directly undermining these. But, it was pointed out, the deduction for trade union subscriptions would be alongside a whole range of others made to wages and salaries. Employees would see deductions for tax and national insurance, alongside possible repayments of student loans, and perhaps payment for an employers' loan scheme, charitable payments, and government schemes for bicycle purchase. The payment of trade union subscription would be based on the same system and an addition at minimal extra cost.

In the announcement there were other hints at 'modernisation' beyond the switch to direct debit over check-off for trade union subscription. The government argued that this would result in a much more direct relationship between the trade union and its membership. It occasionally seems, in their promotion of this measure, that the government is arguing for a return to days when the workplace representative would visit all union members to collect weekly dues and, at the same time, hear the issues concerning members. Hancock argued that by 'ending check-off we are bringing greater transparency to employees – making it easier for them to choose whether or not to pay subscriptions and which union to join.' Thus members, or potential members, are not just given the choice of whether to join or not to join a union but also, to join any union – registered or unregistered – that they might fancy whether recognised by the employer or not. Not only does this measure tear-up voluntary collective agreements entered into by public sector employers and trade unions, but indicates a 'free market' in trade union membership and services. At root, the neo-liberal belief is that the only legitimate purpose of trade unions – as a form of friendly society – is as provider of welfare services to members.

The government introduced its amendment for the 'prohibition on deduction of union subscriptions from wages in public sector.' The measure was scrutinised by MPs at committee stage where witnesses could be called. Under questioning from members of the committee, the spokesman for the Taxpayers' Alliance claimed that the trade unions were receiving hundreds of millions of pounds in subsidy from the government, including millions of pounds from check-off. He was, however, decidedly vague about the calculation of these costs.[73]

More well informed were the union witnesses. Unison, potentially worst hit by an end to public sector check-off, indicated that they had 9,334 voluntary check-off agreements of which 7,242 were with public sector employers, and that 'in many cases we pay an administrative fee or levy to employers to cover the cost and in some cases the fee raises valuable extra revenue for the public body over and above the actual cost, which is small.'[74]

For example, based on exactly the same system and at little or no extra cost, often low paid workers for local government and the NHS, had a simple means of trade union payment: East Lancashire Hospitals NHS Trust, which levied 5% of union subscriptions collected, or Bradford City Council, which received £38,000 a year from their agreement with Unite.[75] Not only did the ILO suggest that an end to check-off arrangements might 'lead to financial difficulties for trade union organizations, (and) is not conducive to the development of harmonious industrial relations and should thus be avoided'[76] but many of the target authorities argued that this would harm the healthy working relationship they had with trade unions, many talking about 'partnership'.

After considerable debate the Bill was amended to contain Clause 15 (see Box 3.17) which allowed the continuance of check-off as long as the trade union member has another possible means of paying union fees, and that the union pays a 'reasonable' amount to cover the

> ## Box 3.17
>
> *Clause 15: Restriction on deduction of union subscriptions from wages in the public sector*
>
> A relevant public sector employer may make deductions from its workers' wages in respect of trade union subscriptions only if—
> (a) those workers have the option to pay their trade union subscriptions by other means, and
> (b) arrangements have been made for the union to make reasonable payments to the employer in respect of the making of the deductions.

administrative cost of making the deduction from payroll.

As a postscript to this saga, within days of the Trade Union Bill being passed into law a High Court Judge ruled that the removal of the deduction by the civil service at the Department of Work and Pensions – the initial move on which the measure in the Bill had been premised – was itself unlawful. The deduction was ruled contractual and should not have been ended without the agreement of the union. Similar action was being pursued against other civil service departments which had unilaterally ended check-off.[77]

5. The Role of the Certification Officer

One feature of the *Trade Union Act* has been the dramatic extension of the role of the Certification Officer (CO) for Trade Unions and Employers Associations. Under the Act, the CO has moved from being a registrar of bodies – with admittedly some limited investigative powers – to becoming the regulator, and more, of the trade unions (see Appendix 3). Established, along with Acas, under the *Employment Protection Act of 1975* to certify and maintain a register of independent trade unions and employers' associations, the Certification Officer has 'been a respected figure'[78] among both sides of industry. In exchange for some tax and other advantages including immunity from tort – civil wrong – during a trade dispute, unions submit annual returns indicating their membership, principal officers and a financial statement. Following reform in the 1980s the CO may, on their own initiative, investigate any financial irregularities within trade unions if there is some suspicion of fraudulent

Box 3.18

Clause 16: Certification Officer not subject to ministerial direction

'(CO) is not subject to directions of any kind from any Minister of the Crown as to the manner in which he is to exercise his functions'

activity. Such investigations are very rare. The CO can also carry out investigations into union finance, elections, and breach of rules, if there has been a complaint by a member of the union. Such complaints can be vexatious, tied to some bitter internal disputes within unions. But, as the Institute of Employment Rights (IER) indicates:

> 'the Trade Union Bill legislates to sway the balance of power in such a way that the regulator become judge, jury and executor. Under Tory proposals, the CO will be able to investigate unions even if no complaints are made against them, fine them for anything judged by the CO to be a breach, and then charged for the process!'[79]

Some changes to the role of the CO have already been noted in the preceding measures of the Act, particularly in the reporting requirements. The CO is now to receive reports of any industrial action, and the nature of that action, taken by members of the union in the preceding year in each annual return. It will also be required to confirm the results of ballots calling for action and that the ballot fulfilled the necessary thresholds stipulated in the Act. The CO will also be responsible for monitoring the use of political funds, with the annual return also containing details of spending over £2,000 in total.

Box 3.19

Clause 17: Investigatory powers etc

'to enable the Certification Officer to exercise certain powers without an application or complaint being made to the Officer, ...'

Box 3.20

Clause 18: Enforcement by Certification Officer of new annual return requirements

(1) Where the Certification Officer is satisfied that a trade union has failed to comply with any of the requirements ... the Officer may make a declaration to that effect.

(2) Before making such a declaration, the Certification Officer–

(a) may make such enquiries as the Officer thinks fit,

(b) must give the union an opportunity to make written representations, and

(c) may give the union an opportunity to make oral representations.

(3) If the Certification Officer makes a declaration it must specify the provisions with which the union has failed to comply.

(4) Where the Certification Officer makes a declaration and is satisfied–

a) that steps have been taken by the union with a view to remedying the declared failure or securing that a failure of the same or any similar kind does not occur in future, or

(b) that the union has agreed to take such steps, the Officer must specify those steps in the declaration.

(5) Where a declaration is made, the Certification Officer must give reasons in writing for making the declaration.

(6) Where a declaration is made, the Certification Officer must also make an enforcement order unless the Officer considers that to do so would be inappropriate.

(7) An "enforcement order" is an order requiring the union to take such steps to remedy the declared failure, within such period, as may be specified in the order.

(8) Where, having given the union an opportunity to make written representations ... the Certification Officer determines not to make a declaration ... the Officer must give the union notice in writing of that determination.

(9) Where the Certification Officer requests a person to provide information to the Officer in connection with enquiries under this section, the Officer must specify the date by which that information is to be provided.

(10) Where the information is not provided by the specified date, the Certification Officer must proceed with determining whether to make a declaration ... unless the Officer considers that it would be inappropriate to do so.

(11) A declaration made by the Certification Officer under this section may be relied on as if it were a declaration made by the court.

(12) An enforcement order made by the Certification Officer under this section may be enforced by the Officer in the same way as an order of the court.

(13) Where an enforcement order has been made, a person who is a member of the union and was a member at the time it was made is entitled to enforce obedience to the order as if the order had been made on an application by that person.

However, as the IER also indicates, the role of the CO is to be crucially expanded as a regulator. Rather than responding to complaints by members of the union before initiating an investigation, the CO can now do this of their own volition; an investigation in which they 'become judge, jury and executioner.' It is not surprising, therefore, that an important amendment demanded in the House of Lords was that the post be independent of political control. Also new is that the role of the CO is intended to become self-funded with the costs paid for through a levy of trade unions and employers' associations, rather than from the Treasury. The powers are outlined in the Act and in three separate schedules to the Act concerned with the investigatory powers of the CO and the power to impose financial penalties in cases it investigates.

The Act, therefore, gives the CO wider powers to investigate suspected breaches of a whole range of established and new requirements of trade

Box 3.21

Clause 19:

Further powers of Certification Officer where enforcement order made... Power to impose financial penalties

Box 3.22

Clause 20: Power to impose levy

(1) The Secretary of State may by regulations make provision for the Certification Officer to require trade unions and employers' associations ("relevant organisations") to pay a levy to the Officer.

(2) The regulations must require the Certification Officer, in determining the amounts to be levied, to aim to ensure that the total amount levied over any period of three years does not exceed the total amount of the Officers' expenses over that period that are referable to specified functions of the Officer. ...

(3) The regulations may make provision for determining what things count as expenses of the Certification Officer for the purposes of provision ... and may in particular provide for the expenses to be treated as including—

(a) expenses incurred by ACAS in providing staff, accommodation, equipment and other facilities ...

(4) The regulations may provide for the Certification Officer to determine the amount of levy payable by a relevant organisation by reference to specified criteria ...

unions, as well as employers' associations. This now covers all aspects of the political fund, including scrutiny of how the money is spent, elections of union officers, industrial action ballots, union mergers, as well as union membership registers and rules. This is clearly a far tighter regulatory framework than experienced by any other type of organisation, especially ones where members already play a strong democratic role in the scrutiny of affairs. It also creates this strong regulatory framework where there have been few actual complaints of misconduct.[80]

The Act now allows the CO to demand actions from a union following an enforcement order, which has the legal weight of a court order. If a union continues non-compliance with the order, there is provision, in Clause 19, for the CO to impose a fine of up to £20,000, with a minimum of £200 (see Box 3.21 and 3.22). Given that there is provision for the Secretary of State to determine the level of penalty, and that there is provision for penalties for outstanding or non-payment, there is a potential for disputes to escalate with entrenched positions ending with union funds being sequestrated. Given that such powers rest with the

Secretary of State, the explicit independence of the CO may prove irrelevant with the politicisation of industrial disputes and disputes between government and unions.

The CO remains a service provided by Acas, 'an independent Crown Agent', funded by the Department of Business but itself required to charge for some of its services. As with Acas and other state agencies under neoliberalism there has been a policy shift requiring them to become self-financing through charges for their services. This Act removes the CO from state funding and makes the office dependent on a levy of trade unions and employers' associations to cover their costs. The Act makes it incumbent on Acas to assess the cost of the provision of facilities, such as office space, to the CO. The CO is then expected to impose a levy so that 'amounts raised are not more than required to cover the expenses of the Certification Officer's function'.

Finally, the Act provides for the possibility of appeals to an Employment Tribunal against financial penalties imposed by the CO. Specifically, the appeals are not required to be concerned with issues of law but can also be based on issues of fact.

Box 3.23

Clause 21: Rights of appeal not limited to questions of law

Has the effect of amending all relevant clauses of the TULR 1992 to widen the right to appeal to reflect this.

Notes

1. See Living Wage Foundation, http://www.livingwage.org.uk/
2. See the website of the IWGB, https://iwgb.org.uk/
3. The LW, NMW and NLW are very unclear how many hours would be required to achieve the basic subsistence wage
4. Leo McKinstry, "Counter-Strike," *The Spectator*, 11 July 2015
5. Regulatory Policy Committee, *Ballot Thresholds in Important Public Services* (2015)
6. TUC, *Trade Union Bill Will Result in Huge Costs for Unions, Government Impact Assessment Reveals* (Trades Union Congress, 21 January 2016 2016); available from https://www.tuc.org.uk/node/124369
7. BISS, *Ballot Thresholds in Important Public Services Consultation Impact Assessment* (London: Department of Business, Innovation and Skills, 2015), July 2015, para 86
8. Liberty. *Trade Union Bill Represents Major Attack on Civil Liberties in the UK*, Monday 7 September 2015. Available from https://www.liberty-human-rights.org.uk/news/press-releases-and-statements/trade-union-bill-represents-major-attack-civil-liberties-uk.
9. See e.g. Jon Stone, 'Parts of Tory Trade Union Bill Resemble General Franco's Dictatorship, Says Tory MP David Davis,' *The Independent*, 13 September 2015
10. John Monks on the TU Bill- "an Attack on Civil Liberties" (30 December 2015); available from http://www.tradeunionfreedom.co.uk/john-monks-on-the-tu-bill-an-attack-on-civil-liberties/.
11. Legislative Consent Motion not approved by the National Assembly for Wales on Tuesday 26 January 2016
12. Len McCluskey, 'Unions Must Be Able to Fight for Workers – Even If It Means Breaking Bad Laws,' *The Guardian*, 19 March 2015 Republished at http://www.ier.org.uk/blog/unions-must-be-able-fight-workers-even-if-it-means-breaking-bad-laws
13. Andy McSmith, 'Union Leader Threatens Illegal Strikes If Government Tightens Rules on Industrial Action,' *The Independent*, 14 June 2015
14. Organised by the Institute for Employment Rights, People's Assembly, CLASS think-tank, Trade Union Coordinating Group and the Campaign for Trade Union Freedom
15. The Institute of Employment Rights have formulated their own proposal for trade union and employment law, in K.D. Ewing, John Hendy, and Carolyn Jones, *A Manifesto for Labour Law: Towards a*

Comprehensive Revision of Workers' Rights (London: Institute of Employment Rights, 2016)

16. Nick Boles MP, Trade Union Bill: Concessions and Government Amendments at Lords Report (Leaked Letter) (26 January 2016); available from http://www.slideshare.net/tradesunioncongress/leaked-bis-letter-on-trade-union-bill-concessions

17. Para 2.1

18. Para 3.2

19. BIS, *Trade Union Reform: Consultation on Ballot Thresholds in Important Public Services* (London: Department for Business Innovation & Skill, 2015), July 2015

20. Regulatory Policy Committee, *Ballot Thresholds in Important Public Services* (2015)

21. Ralph Darlington and John Dobson, *The Conservative Government's Proposed Strike Ballot Thresholds: The Challenge to the Trade Unions* (Liverpool: Institute of Employment Rights, 2015)

22. BIS, *Trade Union Reform: Consultation on Ballot Thresholds in Important Public Services* (London: Department for Business Innovation & Skill, 2015), July 2015

23. E. P. Thompson, "Sir, Writing by Candlelight," in *Writing by Candlelight* (London: Merlin, 1980), p.39-48

24. BIS, *Trade Union Reform: Consultation on Ballot Thresholds in Important Public Services* (London: Department for Business Innovation & Skill, 2015), July 2015

25. ILO, *Report of the Committee of Experts on the Application of Conventions and Recommendations*: Report III (Part 1) (International Labour Conference, 105th Session, 2016)

26. The Department's reason for failing to provide such guidance for the nuclear industry is interesting given the requirement for trade unions themselves to make judgements around catagorising their members for the purposes of ballots: 'the Department says that the UK's civil nuclear legacy is a major public liability, and that tackling the legacy safely, securely and cost-effectively is a national priority. However, the sector is a complex industry with interdependencies between workforces both within and between sites. It states that the Government are working to understand better these interdependencies, before specifying roles with the sector that should be within the scope of the 40% support threshold and bringing forward regulations.' *House of Lords Secondary Legislation Scrutiny Committee 20th Report of Session 2016–17*, HL Paper, p. 2

27. House of Lords, ibid

28. Bruce Carr QC, Will the Trade Union Bill Help or Hinder Industrial Relations? (2016); available from http://www.devereuxchambers.co.uk/assets/docs/news/trade_union_bil l_bc_1222016.pdf.

29. TULR 1992, para 229

30. To House of Commons Committee on Trade Union Bill, First Sitting, 13th October 2015

31. https://www.openrightsgroup.org/about/

32. Findings of the Open Rights Group Election Observation Mission in Scotland and England (2007), https://www.openrightsgroup.org/wp-content/uploads/org_election_report.pdf

33. HoC Public Bill Committee, Trade Union Bill, Fourth Sitting, Thursday 15 October 2015 (Afternoon), p. 146

34. Hansard (House of Commons), 27th April 2016

35. Nick Boles MP, Trade Union Bill: Concessions and Government Amendments at Lords Report (Leaked Letter) (26 January 2016); published in *Socialist Worker* and available from http://www.slideshare.net/tradesunioncongress/leaked-bis-letter-on-trade-union-bill-concessions

36. https://www.gov.uk/government/news/government-announces-review-into-electronic-voting-for-industrial-action-ballots

37. Para 4, 1 2(B)

38. ONS, *Labour Disputes Annual Article*, 2014 (London: Office for National Statistics, 2015), 16th July 2015

39. BIS, *Equality Analysis of the Trade Union Bill* (London: Department of Business Innovation and Skills, 2015), September, p. 8-9

40. House of Lords, Trade Union Bill: Committee (2nd Day) (10 February 2016); available from http://www.publications.parliament.uk/pa/ld201516/ldhansrd/text/1602 10-0001.htm#160210106000441

41. Clause 8.1.1

42. Nick Boles, cited in Trade Union Bill - Committee Stage Report (London: House of Commons Library, 2015). 5 November 2015

43. Ralph Harris, 'Market Versus State,' in *Towards a Liberal Utopia?* (London: The Institute of Economic Affairs, 2005), p. 272

44. Charles G. Hanson, *Taming the Trade Unions: A Guide to the Thatcher Government's Employment Reforms, 1980-90* (Basingstoke and London: Macmillan in association with the Adam Smith Institute, 1991). P. 93

45. Margaret Thatcher's pride, for instance, in crossing the Grunwick

picket on the bus with non-strikers

46. DBIS, *Code of Practice on Picketing* (London: Department for Business, Energy and Industrial Strategy, 2017), para 48, p. 15

47. Ibid, para 2

48. Perhaps symptomatic of the tone of publication is the comment in the preamble: 'The Code's provision apply equally to men and to women, but for simplicity the masculine pronoun is used throughout.'

49. Ibid, para 25

50. CBI, *Response to the Carr Review of the Law Governing Industrial Disputes* (London: Confederation of British Industry, 2015), July 2014

51. HoC, Trade Union Bill: Public Bill Committee, Third Sitting (Parliamentary Debates, General Committees, 2015), 2015/10/15

52. Peter Lazenby, 'Bosses 'more Anti-Union Than Ever',' *Morning Star*, 1 May 2017. Reported also in Gregor Gall, *The Trade Union Act 2016: What Has Its Impact Been So Far?* (Glasgow: Jimmy Reid Foundation, 2017)

53. BIS, *Trade Union Bill: Consultation on Tackling Intimidation of Non-Striking Workers* (London: Department for Business Innovation & Skill 2015), July 2015, p. 7

54. See e.g. Jon Stone, 'Parts of Tory Trade Union Bill Resemble General Franco's Dictatorship, Says Tory MP David Davis,' *The Independent*, 13 September 2015

55. See evidence to HoC, Trade Union Bill: Public Bill Committee, Third Sitting (Parliamentary Debates, General Committees, 2015), 15 Nov 2015

56. See http://www.legislation.gov.uk/uksi/2003/3319/made

57. 'Trade Bodies Divided Over 'Picketing Code' to Protect Strike-Breakers', *The Recruiter*, 4 November 2015

58. REC, Update - Changes to the Conduct Regulations, (The Recruitment & Employment Confederation, 17 May 2016); available from https://www.rec.uk.com/news-and-policy/policy-update/changes-to-the-conduct-regulations

59. Unite the union in their response to a BERR/BIS consultation on the Conduct of Employment Agencies and Employment Businesses Regulations 2003, held in 2009, pointed to the use of agency workers by employers to replace strikers during the strike by dockers at the Port of Dover

60. Charles G. Hanson, *Taming the Trade Unions: A Guide to the Thatcher Government's Employment Reforms, 1980-90* (Basingstoke and London: Macmillan in association with the Adam Smith Institute, 1991), p. 55

61. John Leopold, 'Trade Unions and the Third Round of Political Fund Review Balloting,' *Industrial Relations Journal* 37, no. 3 (2006)

62. Certification Officer, *Annual Report 2015-2016* (Certification Officer for Trade Unions and Employers' Associations. p. 37

63. House o fLords, Trade Union Bill (Report) (16 March 2016); available from http://www.publications.parliament.uk /pa/ld201516/ldhansrd/text/160316-0001.htm#16031633000944

64. Written Evidence Submitted by the Society of Radiographers (TUB 04) (2015); available from http://www.publications.parliament.uk /pa/cm201516/cmpublic/tradeunion/memo/tub04.htm

65. TU Act para 14.4

66. BERR and CBI&TUC, *Reps in Action: How Workplaces Can Gain from Modern Union Representation* (London: BERR/CBI/TUC, 2009), May 2009

67. BERR, *Workplace Representatives: Government Response to Public Consultation* (London: Department of Trade and Industry (BERR), 2007), Consultation Document, November 2007

68. Written Evidence Submitted By Cllr Julian Bell, Leader, Ealing Council (2015); available from http://www.publications.parliament.uk/ pa/cm201516/cmpublic/tradeunion/memo/tub39.htm

69. Written Evidence Submitted By the Directors of Workforce and Organisational Development, NHS Wales (Tub 40); available from http://www.publications.parliament.uk/pa/cm201516/cmpublic/tradeun ion/memo/tub40.htm

70. Gregor Gall, *The Benefits of Paid Time Off for Trade Union Representatives* (London: Trade Union Congress, 2016)

71. Rajeev Syal and agency, 'PCS Union Funding Fears as Government Plans Withdrawal of Direct Payment', *The Guardian*, 19 January 2015

72. Matt Hancock, New Steps to Tackle Taxpayer-Funded Support to Trade Unions', (Cabinet Office, Department for Business, Innovation & Skills and The Rt Hon Matt Hancock MP, 2015/08/06); available from https://www.gov.uk/government/news/new-steps-to-tackle-taxpayer-funded-support-to-trade-unions

73. Jonathan Isaby, to Trade Union Bill Committee, Tuesday 13 October 2015 (Afternoon), available at: http://www.publications. parliament.uk/pa/cm201516/cmpublic/tradeunion/151013/pm/151013s0 1.htm

74. Further Written Evidence Submitted by Unison (Tub 38) (2015); available from http://www.publications.parliament.uk/pa/cm201516 /cmpublic/tradeunion/memo/tub38.htm

75. Ibid

76. ILO, Report of the Committee of Experts on the Application of Conventions and Recommendations: Report Iii (Part 1) (International Labour Conference, 105th Session, 2016)

77. See PCS People Issue 2, 2016

78. IER, 'Tory Peer Backs E-Balloting and Check-Off for Trade Unions' (The Institute of Employment Rights, 2016); available from http://www.ier.org.uk/news/tory-peer-backs-e-balloting-and-check-trade-unions

79. Ibid

80. This can be substantiated through reference to past reports of the Certification Officer found at https://www.gov.uk/government/organisations/certification-officer

81. Certification Officer, *Annual Report 2015-2016* (Certification Officer for Trade Unions and Employers' Associations), p. 2

82. Ibid, p. 3

Chapter 4
Flexing the Kettle?

The *Trade Union Bill*, having passed all its Parliamentary stages, received Royal Assent on 4th May 2016. Most of the new Act came into force on 1st March 2017, principally those parts relating to industrial action ballots. Only time will tell the full impact of the Act, designed by its architects to restrict industrial action and contain the activities of trade unions. It might be several years before any picture of its full impact develops. Any examination, at this stage, can only be a brief snapshot of developments and events. Despite the Act, disputes and conflicts in work and employment have continued, some rooted in issues which emerged long before the passing of the Bill. Employment for many remains precarious, maybe for an increasing number. Those in work face a continuing decline in the value of their take home pay while the pressures and stresses of their work increase as employers seek more ways to reduce costs. The unemployed or casually employed, including the bogus 'self-employed', are pressured by the increasing withdrawal of the state from welfare into becoming the vanguard in advancing the market economy.

A 'winter of discontent'?

The Act has not been defeated before it entered the statute book, like Labour's proposal for *In Place of Strife*, although it might still be undermined and neutered like Heath's Conservative Government's *Industrial Relations Act*. There is a promise that the TU Act will be repealed by an incoming Labour government, the formal fate of Heath's Act, and replaced by a framework of employment and trade union rights. This won't occur without mobilisation and debate.

Although prediction is difficult, there are certainly signs of a new strike wave. It could be that the Office of National Statistics (ONS) continues to report historic lows in the level of industrial action despite a few sectional difficulties. There are also signs that discontent with wages and general conditions might be leading to action. There are indications from trade union leaders of plans for a concerted challenge to the public sector pay cap, with Len McCluskey repeating his willingness to break the law if necessary.[1] In an attempt to neuter this the government has made noises about loosening the pay cap, for example in March 2018 announcing a 6.5% pay increase for NHS staff over three years. Their attempt to present this as a far larger increase for some, as much as 29% for some of the more junior staff,[2] only recognised advancement on already existing incremental pay scales. Like other 'employment costs' to employers, the notion of a progressive pay scale appears under attack. While the announced pay rise is the government's attempt to avert industrial action in the NHS, it is not clear how successful this might be, nor whether this might not add to militancy elsewhere. At their conference in March 2018, teachers in the NUT section of the NEU committed to holding a ballot on industrial action over pay, which is likely to be the first ballot which will not only require the 50 per cent turnout but will also have to meet the 40% threshold for 'important public services' required in the Act.

While conditions are very different to 1978-9 some, including sections of the press, are seeing potential signs of a 'winter of discontent' with an explosion of militancy. Rubbish piled in the streets becomes a powerful metaphor for the inability of the system to cope with everyday needs. Such symbols are accumulating, not least in the recent strikes by refuse workers in Birmingham.[3] Trying to compare current events with the past, to draw parallels with the 1970s, perhaps also misses some nuances of industrial relations. Things are very different to the 1970s and 80s, and conflict is likely to be expressed very differently. The nature of work, the unions, and of industrial action have all drastically changed in the decades since. Industry-wide, all-out, withdrawal of labour, as witnessed in the miners' strike of 1984-5 – itself relatively unique – was never a common model of industrial action. Now industrial action tends to be used far more strategically in targeted short action, rather than informal walk-outs let alone 'fights to the death' struggles. There is usually some compromise reached, which at least appeases the different sides of the dispute, without fundamentally resolving their differences. The still well organised public sector might present a more realistic battlefield. However, in times of revival of militancy it is often the new, as yet unorganised sectors of the economy, which prove important.

In this section we can at least examine developments since the passing of the Act, with some prediction for the future. First there is the remaining implementation of the Act, with the review of electronic ballots, the role of the Certification Officer, and the opposition from the Welsh Assembly, before looking at some disputes following the introduction of the Act, and some possible directions of travel. We can then examine some new and continuing disputes in sectors with long and established union organisation and traditions of militancy. We can also examine a growing unionisation amongst workers in precarious employment, previously considered to be unorganisable, and far from militant. On this basis we might assess the impact of the Act on the capacity of workers to organise and take industrial action.

Implementing the Act

A central concession to the opponents of the Bill, and an attempt to appease the unions, was the establishment of an enquiry into the use of electronic balloting. The government had insisted that industrial action ballots were somehow different from any other form of ballot which could be acceptable electronically – including the use within the Conservative Party - and were insisting on the continuance of postal ballots. There was suspicion that this was a deliberate stance, intended to pass significant cost onto the unions, especially with the need to repeat such a ballot if the dispute was not resolved. An *Independent Review of Electronic Balloting for Industrial Action* was established, chaired by a former advisor on fire and rescue, which reported at the end of 2017. Rather than a recommendation to move to e-balloting – the move made in many other spheres – Sir Ken Knight was more reserved:

'e-balloting in the context that some are proposing to use it is not yet sufficiently tested and assured. To move ahead without that assurance runs a real risk of e-balloting being found to be flawed and therefore not trusted … an early failure would cause significant disruption arising from flawed ballot decisions and would be likely to trigger the withdrawal and delay of e-balloting for many years.'[4]

Instead the review proposes further testing of e-balloting on non-statutory ballots before any decision can be made. At the time of writing, about two months after the publication of the report, there has been no response from the Department for Business, Energy and Industrial Strategy. In March 2018, thirty one MPs, from Labour, SNP, Plaid Cymru and the Green Party, signed an early day motion to the House of Commons arguing that:

'electronic voting is now commonplace for elections in a wide variety of elections in civil society bodies, including the internal elections for the Conservative candidate for Mayor of London and in shareholder ballots of multinational companies; rejects the argument that additional trials are necessary in non-statutory contexts before such widely adopted measures might be employed for industrial action balloting; regrets the Government's unwarranted delay in approving the use of new technologies; fears this is politically motivated and aimed at keeping turnout figures below the arbitrary thresholds imposed in the Trade Union Act 2016; and calls on the Government to expedite the introduction of the latest technology for fair and secure electoral participation as a matter of urgency.'[5]

Important clauses in the Act dealt with the extension of the powers of the Certification Officer (CO) in attempting to kettle the unions. The CO has also become responsible for monitoring the procedure for new members opting into, and the expenditure from, trade union political funds. While these requirements commenced on 1st March 2017, because of transition arrangements, there will be no impact until 2019. Perhaps most importantly, Clauses 16-21 of the Act detail the CO's new powers to initiate investigations rather than react to complaints from trade union members. Following the passing of the Act the retiring incumbent CO voiced his criticisms of this new power. In his final Annual Report, David Cockburn stated that he was never consulted on the new powers or 'whether I had evidence of an unmet demand for further powers prior to the introduction of the Bill.' Of these new powers for the CO introduced in the Act, and for the changed position of trade unions, he voiced fundamental disagreement in principal:

'The regulation of the internal affairs of trade unions has hitherto been based on the premise that they are voluntary associations. Historically, the law has intervened to protect and support the position of members. Thus it is the members who have the right to complain to the Certification Officer about an alleged breach of their rights under the rules of the union or an alleged breach of statute. The Trade Union Act is based on a different premise, namely that the public has an interest in the internal affairs of trade unions given the impact of some industrial action on the public. Accordingly, the right of the Certification Officer to investigate and initiate formal complaints against trade unions has been extended. The role of the Certification Officer will change from being mainly the adjudicator of members' complaints to become one with more general policing and enforcing responsibilities. This is not the role to which I was appointed in 2001.'[6]

The powers given to the office, for the 'investigation and determination of breaches of statutory provisions without a complaint from a member and increased penalty and enforcement powers',[7] had also not themselves been given a commencement date by the Secretary of State. In January 2018, a permanent replacement was found for the post of CO. Instead of an employment lawyer, the usual background for the position, the new CO appears to come from a career as a regulator within the health service.

In May 2016 the Recruitment & Employment Confederation, announced a range of changes to their conduct regulations, but added that:

> 'On 4th May 2016, the Trade Union Bill received Royal Assent. The proposal to remove Regulation 7 is however subject to secondary legislation and so was not mentioned in what is now the Trade Union Act. We have been advised that the next steps for Reg 7 are still under consideration by government and we will keep members informed.'[8]

As yet there appears no action by government ministers to change regulation 7 of the code covering employment businesses, allowing them to supply permanent replacement for workers on strike.

The Welsh Assembly, noting that the UK Government were yet to change the regulations, have made their own 'provision to preserve the prohibition currently in place on the use of agency workers, by employers, to cover staff during periods of authorised industrial action.'[9] Action by the Assembly went further with the passing of their own measure, *Trade Union (Wales) Act,* which uses their available powers to undermine some aspects of the TU Act in the province: 'reversing the adverse effects of the provisions within the UK TU Act, with the aim of protecting the continued delivery of public services in Wales.' As well as disapplying the requirement for the 40 per-cent threshold for industrial action ballots in 'important public services', they will now not apply the power on deduction of union subscriptions or the publication and possible limitation of facilities time for public sector workers.[10]

Testing the Trade Union Act

Two clauses of the Act have been tested in court, where employers have attempted to use it to gain injunctions against industrial action ballots. Argos challenged a strike ballot of its workers carried out by Unite, based on the requirement that the ballot paper must include a summary of the issues in the dispute. The court ruled that a summary had to be a reasonable summary of the dispute but need be no more than that. While the Institute of Employment Rights (IER) considered that unions shouldn't have difficulty in complying with this provision,[11] it is unlikely that this will be the last time a ballot paper is challenged on these grounds. In the other ruling, the requirement to state when any action is likely to take place was the basis of the challenge. In a case brought against BALPA, which represented its pilots, Thomas Cook Airlines challenged the ballot paper which stated that action would be 'on dates to be announced'. The court recognised the complexity of collective bargaining, which the framers of the Bill either missed or ignored its intent to allow employers time to counter any withdrawal of labour. The judge ruled that 'one thing which the subsection does not require the trade union to do is to identify specific dates on which industrial action is to be taken, rather than the period within which it is expected to take place.'[12]

Assessing the potential impact of the Act, or the immediate future of employment relations calls for some speculation. In a very early attempt to assess the impact of the 2016 *Trade Union Act* on trade unions and industrial action, Gregor Gall, a prolific analyst of politics and employment relations, has speculated on twenty possible scenarios 'from which to establish ... the probable impact of the stipulated provisions upon the attitudes and behaviour of workers, their unions and employers.'[13] The measures might reduce the number of strikes because groups of workers are unable to meet the new thresholds, but this might itself lead to increased unofficial action amongst these same groups. Employers might extend disputes to see ballot results as a guide to the feelings of their employees before coming to the bargaining table, or might use the extended period of notice to undermine the effectiveness of any industrial action (See Box 4.1 for full list of scenarios). Of course, any developments will be due to the activities of trade unions and workers as well as employers, and the impact could be very mixed building on the nature of existing relations between them. Even where there might be 'good relations' between unions and employers, the partnerships often stressed by local authorities in their evidence to the *Trade Union Act* Parliamentary Committee, these might become strained by unions not responding quickly to the mood or sentiment of their members or by economies or the impact of government spending cuts. However, local authorities might be unwilling to seek injunctions against their own employees. This might not be the case with some smaller private sector employers. Often the test of legislation comes from small or 'rogue' employers; this was the case, for example with George Ward at Grunwick who challenged trade union recognition and Eddie Shah at Today Newspapers in breaking the print unions, acting as the vanguard

Box 4.1 Gall's Possible Scenarios for the Impact of the Trade Union Act 2016

• There will be fewer strikes and cases of (industrial action short of strike) IASoS because many balloted bargaining groups of members cannot attain the new thresholds.
• Some unions will attain the new thresholds because of tighter organisation, higher levels of occupational and union identity and greater campaigning resources.
• Unions will only select members with strategic power (revenue collection, just-in-time systems) in 'smart strikes'.
• Unions will only ballot their strongest members so that ballots will be won but the extent and degree of leverage generated will be less than before.
• Public sector strikes – essentially political and not economic strikes – will cease to generate political leverage as they are no longer national strikes as national ballots are unlikely to be won.
• Unions will organise more ballots than before to avoid calling single national ballots ... they will ballot areas and regions of membership more selectively so that the risk of losing is lessened.
• Unions will call more action and in truncated periods because of the reduced mandate length so one-day strikes will no longer predominate. This means they will 'front load' action so that dispute escalate more rapidly.
• Workers denied the ability to ballot by their union or not attaining the new thresholds will display an increased propensity to take

unofficial action.
* Aggrieved workers, especially nominally self- employed workers, will increasingly act outside the union movement by maintaining non-membership to avoid being bound by the Trade Union Act in

regard of the balloting, notification and mandate provisions.
* The frequency of IASoS to strikes will increase as sacrifices in earnings are less, helping increase the chances of gaining a mandate for action.
* Other action like pickets, protests and social media campaigns will grow when industrial action is not possible due to inability to meet the new thresholds.
* Employers will wait to see ballot results before being prepared to negotiate, thus extending the length of some disputes ... ballots results will provide more leverage than before because they will have attained a new legitimacy.
* Ballots which produce mandates which just exceed the new thresholds will be more subject to applications for injunctions by employers.
* Employers will be able to undertake more effective counter-preparations given the two-week period of notice so that the effectiveness of strike and IASOS will decline.
* Owing to differing political complexions and distribution of powers, there will be significant regional variations given employment law is devolved to Northern Ireland (where the Trade Union Act does not apply), that the Welsh Assembly Government has begun moves to exempt public services in Wales from being covered by the Trade Union Act 2016 and the Scottish Government has indicated it will not seek to apply the new thresholds where it is the employer. Some Labour-controlled local authorities may also not seek the need thresholds abided by.
* Longer resolution and non-resolution of disputes will have deleterious consequences for morale, productivity and staff turnover because of lingering malcontent amongst workers.
* Quicker resolution through enhanced ballot legitimacy and front-loaded action will have positive consequences for morale, productivity and staff turnover as result of the ending of malcontent.
* Some unions will engage in more concession bargaining and partnership working because their weakened position means they

cannot generate sufficient bargaining power from their reduced ability to take either any industrial action or sufficiently widespread industrial action.
• Some sectors of the economy will be little affected by the new thresholds because of a low propensity to take industrial action because of the prevalence of partnership agreements.
• The availability of electronic balloting will increase unions' ability to pass the new thresholds.

Taken from Gregor Gall, *The Trade Union Act 2016: What Has Its Impact Been So Far?* (Glasgow: Jimmy Reid Foundation, 2017), slightly summarised.

for the Murdoch press and other papers. Importantly, the impact of the Act will also depend on the attitude and behaviour of the courts in ruling on applications for injunctions under the Act: how will courts interpret the requirements on balloting, on the behaviour of pickets, and the other areas where they might have to rule?

Immediate Impact of the Act

Conflict endures, with some long running disputes continuing from before the passing of the Act, with breakdown in bargaining and periodic industrial action without ballots under the new rules. Some ballots have also been held since the Act came into force, with differing impacts of the new legislation. While some have achieved the thresholds on both the majority and turnout, like security officers at London University, organised by the IWGB, who achieved 100% support for industrial action in their ballot.[14] Gregor Gall reports four ballots which failed the threshold for turnout while achieving a majority of those voting (see Box 4.2). The most significant of these was, perhaps, the ballot by Unison of Scottish local government workers, where 63% voted for industrial action with a turnout of only 23% in a challenge to the governments pay cap.[15] Any explanations for why the turnout was so low must be left to speculation. It may have been apathy, or just acquiescence of local government workers i.e. that they were not able to challenge the government's 1% pay cap on their own. Alternatively, it could have been caused by problems in the arrangements for the ballot. It might have been that the workers felt that the employers would settle for the 1%

Box 4.2: Industrial Action Ballots: April to June 2017

i) Thresholds reached

Of the ballots conducted since 1 March 2017, for which full figures have been released:

• NUT members in two north London schools voted by 100% on 86% and 90% turnouts.

• Unite's British Airways 'mixed fleet' cabin crew members voted by 91% on a 69% turnout for strike action.

• EIS FELA members voted by 96% for strike action on a 59% turnout.2

• 3,500 Unite BMW members voted 93% for strike action and 97% for industrial action short of strike action on a 72% turnout.

• RMT London Underground Night Tube members 97% for striking and 98% for IASOS on a 100% turnout.

• RMT London Underground London Bridge members 92% for striking and 87% for IASOS on a 58% turnout.

• RMT Arriva Traincare members 96% for striking and 98% for IASOS on a 61% turnout.

• Unite's 1400 Argos members voted 85% voted for strike action on a 73% turnout.

ii) Thresholds not reached

Four ballots for strike action and IASOS have been lost:

• RMT London Underground Waterloo
75% for striking and 94% for IASOS on a 48% turnout.

• RMT Stagecoach South West
48% for striking and 65% for IASOS on a 48% turnout.

• UNISON's ballot of Scottish local government workers
63% vote in favour of industrial action on a 23% turnout.

• RMT London Underground
3,743 members were balloted with an 80% vote for strike action and an 87% vote IASOS on a 34% turnout.

Taken from: Gregor Gall, *The Trade Union Act 2016: What Has Its Impact Been So Far?* (Glasgow: Jimmy Reid Foundation, 2017).

anyway, with a meeting with local government employers already arranged for after the ballot result. In some cases it might be that, despite the low incidence of industrial action generally, particular groups remain embroiled in long running disputes and might feel 'industrial action fatigue' either because of the intransigence of employers, or because of frequent pay losses due to periodic days of strike action.

Such long-term conflict accounts for a high incidence of ballots amongst railway workers, particularly on London Underground. In 2015, two years before the implementation of the Act, London Underground workers took industrial action over the lack of real consultation on the implications of 24-hour working, on loss of staff – particularly around the closure of ticket offices – as well as the outsourcing of work and other issues. Other disputes occurring after the Act have roots much earlier. In 2010, and challenged by the unions in the courts,[16] BA established a 'mixed fleet' of new staff, appointed on poorer conditions than existing staff. The cabin crew complained about low pay, with salaries as low as £16,000, and the need to supplement this income by using food banks. They staged escalating strike action, of 1-, 2- and 3-day strikes, amounting to 86 days in total without settlement up to September 2017.[17] BA management had leased planes from Qatar Airlines to replace their own services lost in strike action. There was also suggestion by BA management of moving all staff to a far less generous pension scheme.[18]

Neoliberalism, increasingly penetrating management thinking, identified labour as a cost rather than as the actual creative source of goods and services. 'Human resources' were but one expense which needed to be purchased rather than itself being productive of value. Instead, reward was transferred to senior managers, presented as the mystical creators of wealth for shareholders through their innovative and strategic thinking. The cost of employment was opened to scrutiny, in new management methods, becoming subject to dramatic economies with the effect of reducing the overall income to those employed. Unproductive hours were squeezed from the working day or night and payment for unsocial hours, the premium paid for working nights, weekends, and public holidays, were eroded. Behind the new and continuing disputes, we might see four, often interrelated, factors involved in the underlying conflict:

1. Changes to pensions, with employers reducing their costs by switching from final salary to fixed benefit schemes, with subsequent

loss to scheme members;

2. Long established employers attempting to introduce a deterioration in terms and conditions of employment, often on the grounds of competition from cheaper suppliers;

3. organisation of precarious workers, often but not exclusively by 'new unions' such as the IWGB, against conditions of precarious labour such as low pay and bogus self-employment; and

4. mounting conflict over the governments' 1% pay ceiling which has lasted for over seven years, meaning a substantial loss of pay to public sector workers, already often on low pay.

Pension Disputes in the Universities and Royal Mail

A pension scheme had been one of the hallmarks of 'a good job', along with the recognition of trade unions which could fight for and defend all aspects of pay and conditions. With the long attack on unions these schemes have come under attack. However, pension schemes have also been the focus of suspect, if not illegal, practice by employers and others taking advantage of workers contributions. Famous examples include Robert Maxwell, owner of the Mirror Newspaper group who used the funds for his own benefit;[19] through to the much publicised failure of the BHS pension scheme after the store group was sold; members of the British Steel scheme losing out when this was taken over and funds shifted to independent advisors in what was described as a 'major mis-selling scandal'.[20] Not only have these made the trustees of such schemes increasingly trust averse, it has made members and the public increasingly suspicious of their management. Many schemes were closed, thereby saving the employer contribution. The end of 'jobs for life' not only meant increased insecurity in work but also in retirement. Some were converted from providing a pension related to final salary to lump sum provision. Defined benefits schemes, which paid a proportion of salary into retirement, were replaced by defined contributions which pay a lump sum to be invested at retirement, giving an amount dependent on the state of the investment market at the time. This drift escalated following the crash and the low interest rates that followed. Previous surpluses in schemes were reassessed as deficits by actuaries in the post-crash environment, not only because of low interest rates but also with increased threat of failure of any scheme.

Two of the most significant post-Act disputes focussed on changes to occupational pension schemes, occurring at Royal Mail and in Universities operating the Universities Superannuation Scheme.[21] Each dispute – as is common in strikes – had far deeper sources than simply changes to pension schemes. Other issues permeated to the surface. While in neither case did the *Trade Union Act* have significant impact on the direction of the dispute, beyond the requirements of the initial industrial action ballot, they both raised questions of significance for the future pattern of conflict following the Act.

One of the most significant disputes following the *Trade Union Act*, occurred at the Royal Mail. While the Communication Workers Union (CWU), which represents postal workers, held one of the first ballots under the Act and comfortably achieved the threshold, Royal Mail successfully challenged industrial action. This was nothing related to the Act but to a unique, legally binding, agreement between CWU and the Royal Mail signed at the time of privatisation.[22] In the deregulation of postal services, Royal Mail was thrown into competition with alternative providers that deployed all the employment methods of the 'gig economy'. Privatisation had precipitated a 'dash for cash', hitting the terms and conditions of Royal Mail workforce. The CWU Deputy General Secretary, Terry Pullinger, argued that privatisation meant a 'a short term focus on cutting costs to boost shareholder return.'[23] This, he argues,

> 'has led to serious problems in the workplace around resourcing, growing intensification and pressure at work, as well as mounting concerns about the impact of automation, Royal Mail's growth agenda and the long term future of members' jobs, standard of living and retirement security.'[24]

With consultation on the future of pensions, the CWU launched the 'Four Pillars of Security' Campaign bringing together the union concerns into proposals for change. These four pillars were:

- A lasting pension solution that delivers a decent wage in retirement for all members in both the Defined Benefit and Defined Contribution schemes;
- An extension of all our current agreements and legal protections enshrined in the Agenda for Growth Agreement;
- A 35 hour shorter working week to address growing pressures and intensification of work and improve members' health, well-being and work-life balance; and

- A redesigned Royal Mail pipeline to secure the company's commercial future and deliver long term growth.

Part of the CWU campaign was concerned with the decline in working conditions, in part through a chase to the bottom with 'gig economy' delivery services, which had taken an increasing proportion of the market, particularly over the extension of delivery times. Royal Mail had also announced its intention to use new technology, principally the Automated Hours Data Capture (AHDC) technology, to record the hours of work. While Royal Mail claimed resulted from scrutiny by the regulator, Ofcom, the union was concerned that it would be used to control and discipline delivery workers.[25] The union were also concerned that the Royal Mail planned changes to agreements reached with the union which gave workers some representation in discussions of working practices and change.[26] In 2013 the CWU had signed the *Agenda for Growth,*

> 'a ground breaking agreement which for the first time in the UK incorporates unique legal elements into a collective agreement demonstrating our joint commitment to delivering long term success in the interests of customers, employees and the company.'[27]

In exchange for a legally binding agreement, unique in UK industrial relations where such agreements are voluntary (see Section 1), they felt they had achieved protection for their pension scheme as well as terms and conditions for postal workers. With Royal Mail's planned closure of the defined benefit pension, and other changes in the pipline, the CWU thought the legally binding agreement had been broken.[28]

While there was a range of union concerns, the actual spark for industrial action was that, four years after privatisation on 31st March 2018, Royal Mail planned to close its defined benefit pension scheme. The scheme had been closed to new entrants since 2008, who, after a 12-months in the 'nursery section', were placed on a defined contributions scheme. After about 18 months consultation on the future scheme, talks between Royal Mail and the CWU broke down. The union promoted a 'Wage in Retirement Scheme' (WinRS), with the company arguing that 'as a large defined benefit scheme WinRS would be vulnerable to volatility which would impact on the funding of the scheme and, under current accountancy regulations, the Company would quickly be shown as technically insolvent on its balance sheets.'[29]

By mid-August, after about three months of the campaign, the CWU felt some progress had been made on the issue of pay, but:

'there is still no sign of a decent revised pay offer from the company which responds to the CWU's claim for standard of living and income security for our members. Neither is there a resolution on the important issue of holiday pay for part-timers which forms a crucial part of the current pay talks.'[30]

Also, and perhaps more pressing, the negotiations had made no progress on closure of the Defined Benefit pension and the future of the schemes. They seemed deadlocked on the union claim for a single pension, a wage in retirement scheme, available for all Royal Mail employees. According to the CWU:

'Royal Mail are facing two ways on this issue – on the one hand they say our scheme is good and are willing to put money into it, but only if someone else is willing to run it on the company's behalf. If it comes to them running it, suddenly it's a bad scheme. If they cannot agree to the fundamental principle of a new pension scheme for all our members and equally pension provision for all, then we will be in dispute.'[31]

By mid-August, with this deadlock, the union proposed to move to an industrial action ballot. In an unhurried schedule, clearly with the intention of trying to shift Royal Mail into more meaningful negotiation, ballot papers were issued from 14th September with the declaration of the result early in October.

The protracted period of the ballot certainly gave time for possible negotiations to continue and also gave time for the union to continue publicising its case, particularly to the membership who received weekly bulletins as well as briefings from officers. Probably the key rationale of the ballot was for the union to show the strength of feeling of CWU members. With no further negotiation or offer, on 6th October the results were announced: over 89% had voted for industrial action on a turnout of 73.7%, comfortably achieving the thresholds of the *Trade Union Act*; with overwhelming support from the membership the CWU set the first strike day as the 18th October 2017.

On the announcement of the ballot result, and of the dates for industrial action, Royal Mail sought an injunction from the High Court to halt the strike. While very much in the wake of the passing of the *Trade*

Union Act, this action was nothing to do with the legal powers in the Act, but related to the unusual character of Agenda for Growth. The legally binding Agenda for Growth Agreement, which the union and Royal Mail had both signed at the time of privatisation, required that in the case of unresolved disputes, an external mediator is appointed, agreeable to both Royal Mail and the CWU, to 'attempt to facilitate agreement between the parties on the issues in dispute.'[32] Despite union argument that they had been in negotiation for 18 months and reached deadlock, on granting the injunction to halt the action the judge argued that the union 'is obliged to withdraw its strike call until the external mediation process has been exhausted.'[33]

In the four weeks of consultation no agreement was reached, although Lynette Harris, the Acas conciliator agreed by both parties, considered there had been progress and an opening of dialogue.[34]

> 'What was apparent from the process was the importance of there being a continuing dialogue between the parties and the value of an approach based on finding joint solutions in the interests of the business and its workforce. As a result, whilst I am required to address the summary positions of the parties upon specific matters in my report, my final recommendations have also considered the wider issue of joint working.'[35]

Progress was made in discussion of pay and, particularly, it seems, on the issue of the pension scheme. While Royal Mail rejected a continuance of the defined benefit scheme, 'the WinRS scheme was recognised by the Employer to be an innovative proposal and, as a result, it reported investing considerable time exploring its viability.' However, Royal Mail considered it 'vulnerable to volatility which would impact on the funding of the scheme and, under current accountancy regulations, the Company would quickly be shown as technically insolvent on its balance sheets.'[36]

Following conciliation, negotiations continued over the Christmas and New Year period. In early January, in a 20-minute video from Terry Pullinger, Deputy General Secretary- Postal, there were hints that members should 'brace themselves' for a ground-breaking agreement which included pay and a new pension scheme.[37] A week later there were indications that negotiations were continuing but 'we may need to take industrial action'[38] At the end of January the CWU announced that an agreement had been reached with Royal Mail:

As well as a three-year pay deal and two-hour cut in the working week worth 12.33% overall (when linked to the shorter working week), the agreement includes the introduction of a potentially ground-breaking new pension scheme for all Royal Mail employees, which will provide the UK's first collective defined contribution pension and a guaranteed cash lump sum.[39]

A complication was that agreement was based on the government introducing 'collective benefit' schemes – a means of pooling and regularly assessing accrued benefits – which had been proposed in the *Pension Scheme Act 2015* but not yet introduced. Similar agreement was reached covering other workers who had been covered by the Post Office scheme, prior to privatisation.[40] Despite the complexity concerning the basis of the pension scheme but offering what appeared a large pay rise in the current environment, 91% of CWU postal workers voted in favour of agreement.[41]

Perhaps the most public of the disputes concerning pensions was in the Universities. The protracted dispute around the USS pension scheme sheds light on why the issue was headlining many other industrial disputes. In 2017 Universities UK, which represented the management of the Universities, and the Chair of the Board of the USS, announced that the scheme had a £6.1 billion shortfall in funds needed to meet its obligations. This meant they needed not only to change from a predominantly defined benefit to a defined contribution scheme, but also to substantially increase contributions from both University employers and employees to remain viable.[42] The USS scheme had made some significant recent shifts in this direction, moving towards a limit on salary related benefit. The Universities and Colleges Union (UCU) objected to the new proposed changes on the basis that, not only had the scheme previously been considered to be in £8.3bn surplus but that the changes being proposed would result in members losing an estimated £10,000 a year when they drew their pension.

The changes bore no relation to the actual value of the assets held by the USS, but concerned the assessment of future return on the scheme from investments. The valuation of all schemes dependent on investment income had been hit by the low return following the stock market crash. This recent assessment seems related to three factors in the calculation on this return to cover the cost of pensions. Firstly, a majority of the employers indicated a strong aversion to risk in the management of the portfolio, indicating a preponderance of investment in safer government bonds rather than more speculative shareholding. As the dispute progressed it also appeared that the USS/Universities UK position was weighted towards Oxford and Cambridge Colleges which each had an individual vote, rather than individual Universities. Second, return on gilts had declined over the past two years meaning that the assessment of future income from the investment in gilts was dramatically reduced. Finally, and principally because of the failure of schemes such as at BHS where the company collapse led to the redundancy of all staff and major deficit in their pension scheme, the USS deficit was calculated around liabilities in the total failure of the University system.

With the two sides essentially viewing the health of the scheme from fundamentally different vantage points, talks between UUK and UCU were in stalemate. To assess support for industrial action UCU held a 'consultative' ballot of its USS members in November 2017, with a healthy majority supporting an escalation to try to break the deadlock. A formal ballot was held in the new year for strike action and for action short of strikes, with UCU disaggregating to count membership separately at each institution involved in USS. All had a majority voting in favour but, of the 67 included, 6 failed to achieve the required 50% threshold of voting members.

A series of 14 days of escalating strikes were organised for four weeks from late February, with 2 days of action in the first week, 3 in the second, 4 in the third, the full week of strike action in the final week.[43] Increasingly, however, it was clear that the dispute involved more than the value of University pensions. Like other workers, particularly in the public sector, University staff had experienced a decline in real income. In mid-2016 they had staged a strike against a 1.1 per cent pay offer.[44] This austerity was aggravated by escalating pay for Vice Chancellors. As *THES* reported in their sector-wide survey at the time of the strikes:

'vice-chancellors were paid an average of £268,103 in salary, bonuses and benefits. This was £10,180 more than in 2015-16, amounting to a rise of 3.9 per cent. Once employer pension contributions are included, vice-chancellors received a total pay package of £289,756 on average, a rise of 3.2 per cent. Some 13 universities paid their leaders a total of more than £400,000 in 2016-17, while 64 paid more than £300,000.'[45]

Even more, it emerged that the Chief Executive of the USS pension scheme, at the time when they were trying to cut future pension entitlement by £10,000 per annum, had received a 17 per cent pay increase, a rise of £82,000 bringing his salary to £566,000 with two of his staff receiving more than £1million a year each in salary and bonuses.[46]

An important underlying cause of the dipute was the growing casualisation of University employment, with some of the strikers unlikely to ever benefit significantly from the pension scheme they seemed to be fighting for. Many University staff can be included in what has been termed the 'gig economy': working part-time and on short-term engagement on hourly pay, often at two or three separate institutions. A study by UCU had indicated that 'somewhere between 15 and 40% of undergraduate teaching is being delivered by hourly paid staff, with the average being 27%.'[47] At some pre-1992 Universities, those involved in the dispute, up to half the undergraduate teaching could be carried out by hourly paid staff. This also impacted on the career of academic staff, and their eligibility to pensions, with a 'typical academic career trajectory … [which] involves moving from hourly-paid teaching as part of a PhD to hourly-paid teaching as substantive employment, often with another university, with possible fixed-term contracts afterwards.'[48] In this environment pensionable employment might not come until academics reached their thirties or forties, if at all.[49]

Early in the dispute there were attempts to divide students from lecturers, and to perhaps foster division amongst the lecturers themselves. Arguments appeared in the media to the effect that not only might this strike action be severely detrimental to students, through delaying graduation and perhaps impacting on future careers, but that some might claim for the return of fees and possibly damages for lost teaching.[50] Universities considered making deductions from the salary of staff for 'non-fulfilment of duties' associated with the action short of strike, which continued in non-strike days of the dispute, as well as the deduction of salary for days on strike. Instead, there was evidence of student support for the action, not just formally from the National Union of Students (NUS) but also from students joining their lecturers on picket lines. Some also staged occupations in support of the action.[51]

This all indicates that underlying the dispute, mobilising the strike and support, were greater concerns far beyond the immediate USS pension scheme. This mood is captured in the blog of one of the strikers who also talks of his work experience across a number of precarious University jobs:

'There is a long list of other issues including: precarity, pay (and the gender pay gap), institutional sexism and racism, workload modelling that bears little if any relationship to reality, stress and bullying, the pointlessness of REF (a way of comparing research outputs) and TEF (the teaching version), the attempt to make academics act like border officials, racist policies like Prevent, and so on. ... Legally, this strike is about pensions, but it is also clearly about so much more. It is about all the other issues we know are happening at universities, but have not fought over.'[52]

Broadly, the dispute was increasingly seen as one against the 'marketisation' or 'commercialisation' of the Universities with the commodification of education. That in recent years, and symbolised by the introduction of fees to students, the very nature of the University has changed from a 'seat of learning', or perhaps 'community of scholars', into business organisations concerned with income and return on investment.

As the strikes continued it appeared that the Universities were increasingly divided in their response. As it became clear the USS revaluation of the scheme had been influenced by risk averse Oxford Colleges, the Vice Chancellor of Oxford University shifted her position backing a less risk averse recommendation.[53] Some Vice Chancellors had gone further and, in sympathy with their staff, joined the picket lines. With growing fear from the Universities that the strikes might continue into the examination season, talks between UCU and UUK began under the auspices of Acas. After several days of discussion, there was an agreement between the parties for a halting of industrial action and the Universities accepting a slight increase in risk, a three-year transition arrangement including an expert panel who could explore alternative arrangements – including the possible introduction of a Collective Defined Benefits scheme as in the Royal Mail agreement. The agreement also involved increased contributions and less accrued benefits.[54] However, this was little improvement to the initial proposed changes to the pension scheme. It also didn't address the underlying concerns of UCU members, including the strong suspicion that UUK were purely concerned with ending the industrial action, rather than resolving the cause of dispute. This agreement between the UCU and UUK was rejected outright by the membership at union branch meetings.

UCU members agreed a slightly modified proposal from the UUK. The central proposal is the establishment of:

'A formally agreed Joint Expert Panel, comprised of actuarial and academic experts nominated in equal numbers from both sides will be commissioned, to deliver a report. Its task will be to agree key principles to underpin the future joint approach of UUK and UCU to the valuation of the USS fund.'[55]

The proposal seems, at least partially, spurred by the University's attempt to end any action before it has any major impact on examinations. While some UCU members appear willing to accept the expert panel as a means out of the stalemate, others warn that it doesn't resolve the pension issue or address any of the other concerns. The proposal lacks any substance for a final settlement and is, essentially, a 12-month truce in the dispute.[56]

Pensions and the pay cap

Pension disputes have not been exclusive to the public sector. In early 2017, just before the Act came into force, BMW proposed to transfer about 3,500 of its workforce onto a defined contribution scheme which had been operated for new entrants since 2014. Like the BA dispute, this was an attempt to generalise poorer conditions introduced for new starters to all the workforce. Unite, the union, estimated that the proposed changes to the pension scheme would mean some members could lose £160,000 in retirement income. A ballot of Unite members at BMW returned 93% in favour of strike action, with 97% supporting other action. The union announced eight 24-hour strikes through April and May, alongside a ban on overtime and a work-to-rule at the four BMW plants manufacturing and assembling the Mini and Rolls Royce cars. The action prompted BMW to put forward revisions to their scheme and, after suspension of action, enhancement payments were agreed for the transfer.[57]

At the Atomic Weapons Establishment sites at Aldermaston and Burghfield – following privatisation by a consortium consisting of Lockhead Martin, Jacobs Engineering and Serco, but with a notional government 'golden share' allowing it to outvote the other partners – a series of strikes were held by workers objecting to changes to their pension. They finally agreed to the changes in exchange for a 4% annual pay increase for the next three years along with enhancements to allowances for working with hazards and to overtime payments.[58]

In the public sector the issue of pensions was compounded by the pay cap, introduced as part of government austerity measures. The cap pegged pay increases to 1% per annum for more than seven years and, with inflation at about 2.7%, public sector workers endured a substantial pay cut.[59] At the Bank of England itself, maintenance and security workers staged a three-day strike against the pay cap.[60] The announcement of a 1% plus 1% bonus to the police, 1.7% to prison officers with the possibility of easing the cap for other groups like teachers and NHS workers in future reviews, does not seem to be stemming a growing tide. It is as an attempt to avert a growing tide of militancy that a pay offer headlined as worth up to 29% but in practice only about 6.5% over three years, was made by the government to NHS workers.[61]

The national executive of the Public and Commercial Services Union (PCS), representing civil servants, passed a resolution for 'a programme of activities in the run-up to the autumn budget to put pressure on the government to break the pay cap for all public sector workers.'[62] The action was to include a ballot to explore the possibility of industrial action to challenge the pay cap. With pressure building, and the pay cap held tight for almost twice that for the period leading to 1978, it is not surprising that some are beginning to predict a 'winter of discontent'.[63]

Changes in working hours and conditions have also built unresolved conflicts, particularly involving railway workers. Not only have there been changes on London Underground, long running disputes have been endemic in some of the mainline franchises. Southern Railways has come to symbolise this with frequent disruption to services. While there have been a range of problems, in terms of employment relations, most have stemmed from the company's attempt to introduce driver-only trains, replacing the conductor's role in safety by remote CCTV from the driver's cab. The more than twelve months of periodic days off through strike action result from the lack of engagement with the workforce, attempting to steamroll through changes. The general secretary of the National Union of Rail, Maritime and Transport (RMT), Mick Cash, voiced disappointment in August 2017, at the start of a series of further one-day strikes, stating that he was: 'bitterly disappointed that Southern Rail have rejected our call for round-table discussion: involving all parties with an interest in resolving this dispute.'[64]

Conflict in the 'new economy': organising the unorganised?

It is not just that pay and conditions are deteriorating in established sectors of the economy, like the railways. New, or expanding, sectors are leading a spiralling downwards in a cost cutting drive. Low paid workers have begun to mobilise for pay increases and improved conditions. This has been evident amongst contract cleaners and other ancillary workers, employed through agencies, but also seen amongst direct employees. Workers at Ritzy Cinemas continue to spread their long-standing action for a living wage and sick pay, as well as defence of union organisation.[65]

Box 4.3: Number (thousands) of people in employment reporting they are on a zero hours contract, 2000 to 2017

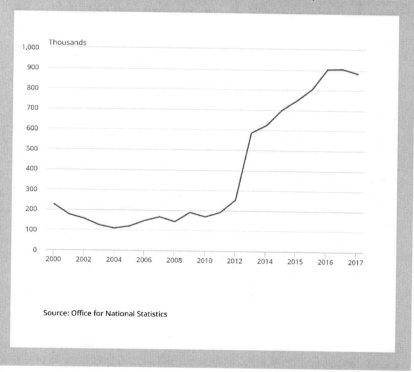

Source: Office for National Statistics

Precarious work, symbolised by zero-hours contracts and bogus 'self-employment' as well as tightly controlled and intensive work routines, has been drawn into the mainstream by job creation in the 'new economy'. Government estimates are that almost 900,000 workers are on zero-hours contracts, almost certainly an underestimate, and a four-fold increase on the figure since the year 2000 (see Box 4.3). While accounting for only about 5% of the workforce, this is highly concentrated in some areas, particularly those with a high proportion of women employed. So in the three months to June 2017, official figures indicate that of those on zero-hours contracts, '23.1% worked in health and social work, and 21.1% worked in the accommodation and food sector.'[66] Self-employment has also grown by close to 50%, with official figures of almost 5 million. Evidence is that conditions for the new self-employed are not comparable to traditional sectors of self-employment, income being consistently below those for the directly employed. Even the government's own account of the income of the self-employed puts their median income, in 2013/14, as only £10,800 compared to that of the employed at £20,000.[67]

Growth in private sector jobs has been characterised as 'McJobs',[68] not just in the burgeoning fast food sector but also in warehousing, call centres, and other sectors of the 'new economy'. Union organisation, and industrial action, have begun to spread to areas hard pressed by low pay and poor conditions but considered too casual and fragmented to organise. On 4th September 2017 workers at two McDonalds UK outlets, in Cambridge and in South London, staged a one-day strike following a near unanimous ballot of their 40 workers. This followed a recruitment campaign by the Bakers, Food and Allied Workers Union (BFAWU) modelled on the work of union organisers in the USA.[69] Workers complained about the uncertain hours and low wages, and demanded £10 an hour.[70]

Sports Direct has become emblematic of employment practices in the new economy. Symbolically, its headquarters and the vast warehouse feeding its national chain of stores selling cheap branded goods, is built on the redeveloped site of the Shirebrook colliery. The colliery closed in 1993 following record output for the North Derbyshire Area in the year 1986/7.[71] In 2016, following scathing publicity from investigative journalists in the press and television, a Parliamentary Select Committee investigated working conditions at the company. The chair of the committee said the 'evidence we heard points to a business whose working practices are closer to that of a Victorian workhouse than that of a modern, reputable High Street retailer.'[72] Evidence the committee heard showed that workers were penalised for taking even short breaks to drink water, for taking time off sick – with stories of a woman worker having given birth in the warehouse toilets rather than take time-off. The company had a 'six strikes and you're out' policy for staff, so all transgressions, however minor, could lead to dismissal. In this regime most of the, largely migrant, workforce from Eastern Europe were employed indirectly on zero-hours contracts through one of two employment agencies. Some workers had been promised full time jobs by supervisors in exchange for sexual favours. For this they were working below minimum wage because of unpaid time spent in security checks at the warehouse.[73] While Mike Ashley, the CEO of Sports Direct, had promised the committee that employment and working practices would be improved, a year later little has changed. However, on clocking-on, workers were required to press a button with either a smiling or frowning emoji to indicate their mood. If they indicate that they are unhappy then they are required to 'explain themselves' to a manager.[74]

The condition of 'self-employed contractors' at the beck-and-call of an employing company has been dubbed the 'Uber economy', after the taxi company which links driver and customer through a smart phone app. Others, such as delivery companies, use similar technologies. Some have also called it the 'gig economy', a reference to the employment of many musicians and actors who move from one paid engagement to another in what can be a life of 'feast and famine' dependent on the flow of work. While mediated by new technology this appears to be a return to the summoning of servants: the ring of the household bell replaced by the smartphone. In 2016, in a case of two Uber drivers, brought by the General, Municipal and Boilermakers Union (GMB), an employment tribunal ruled that drivers were employees and therefore entitled to the national minimum wage as well as holiday and sick pay. There were claims from drivers that, designated as self-employed, they were not only earning around £5 an hour but that the company made punative fines and deductions for minor contraventions of Uber rules.[75] A similar ruling has been made in the case of drivers for Addison Lee, another taxi company.[76]

In recognition that the 'labour market is changing, self-employment is rising, innovative forms of working are causing us to question established norms and how our current legislative framework fits with these developments' and that 'these changes have impacts for ordinary people, who may be less certain about their rights, or who might feel that the system doesn't accommodate the reality of their working relationships,'[77] Theresa May established a review into the new working arrangements chaired by Mather Taylor. The 'Taylor Review' was described as 'not the game-changer needed to end insecurity at work'[78] by the TUC, the report largely neutralised the new employment practices by describing 'dependent contractors' involved in 'platform-based working.'[79]

While defined by companies as self-employed contractors to keep them isolated and individualised, there has been some challenge from these workers including unionisation and industrial action. Challenging the company changes to the payment system, Deliveroo couriers took action in August 2016, organised by the IWGB.[80] As part of the action they staged a protest at the company head office in London.

'The negotiations ended with Deliveroo saying that it would be impossible to increase wages. This was met with anger by the drivers who promptly voted to go and visit some of the restaurants Deliveroo works with and return to the headquarters the next day. Over the megaphone someone shouted "it's only impossible until we win!" And with that a convoy of hundreds of mopeds set off into central London.'[81]

While there is controversy concerning the self-employed status of workers at companies like Deliveroo and Uber, where the individualised control of 'self-employed' contractors through a smartphone app is central to the very company ethos, it does raise a catch-22 in terms of industrial action not yet tested in court.

Clearly, the delivery riders for Deliveroo appear to be taking part in industrial action. But the nature of being 'self-employed contractors' through the use of a smartphone app, and its inherent informality, makes the use of leverage tactics like the protest at the Deliveroo headquarters more likely than more formal picketing and organised disputes. The insistence of the company that they would not see union representatives but only listen to a delegation of their riders – declined because of possible victimisation – appears a throwback to the beginning of the 20th century. The Taff Vale railway company would not recognise the union, engage in collective bargaining, and would only see a delegation of railway workers. The victimisation of one of the delegation sparked the strike. While the business model might be similar, the level of control exerted in the 21st century using an app is far more draconian than could be exercised over workers in the 20th. The dispute at Taff Vale led to the formal recognition of trade unions, the establishment of the 'golden rule' which allowed immunity from civil action when this arose from a trade dispute, but this recognition has been the subject of the 'kettling' since 1980, with the sustained attack by neoliberals and their promotion of the competitive market. But where does self-employment fit within the framework of the new *Trade Union Act*? A 'gig-economy' company seeking injunction in the case of withdrawal of labour, or other action, would itself appear a recognition of employee status. Would they be able to claim damages caused by such action, particularly if the union concerned had carried out a ballot of members? Any case such as this might imply a recognition of the union.

Recognition in the global economy

Employment status is likely to become an important, if sometimes submerged, issue in future conflicts. And such conflicts are often very complex. In September 2017, Ryanair announced the cancellation of thousands of flights on the budget airline. This was initially blamed on mistakes in rostering pilots' holiday entitlement, but increasingly the problems appeared rooted in employment relations. What quickly emerged was that pilots had been complaining about conditions, particularly concerning annual leave, and sought discussions with Ryanair management. A letter from the pilots to the company argued that:

'As a pilot group we regret that you are not willing to solve the problems Ryanair is facing now. We offered our help, however you prefer to cancel flights and leave the passengers out in the cold. We do not understand why Ryanair management sees us as the enemy when we are actually colleagues.'[82]

While prohibited in their contract from joining a union, a clause allowed under Irish law, the pilots were clearly unionising and had hired a professional negotiator and demanded uniform contracts for pilots across the airline.[83] Unionisation was also spreading to cabin crew whose complaints included low pay, but also that their working time only included time in flight and not that on the ground. The budget airline was squeezing cost from both passengers and staff. As well as pay, with some dependent on in-flight sales, and working time arrangements cabin staff complained about payment for training and for uniforms. They also had to pay for their onboard refreshment when on duty.[84] A Facebook page and other social media were utilised to organise the protest with claims that a coordinated 'sick-day' was being planned, followed by a mass exodus to jobs at another airline. One anonymous member of crew told a *Telegraph* reporter that:

'We have almost 3,000 cabin crew coming together on social media, and we are working on a manifesto, a list of demands. We are not allowed to have a union, and we are not allowed to have a voice, but we are still going to organise, and if they don't listen to us then we will do something. There will come a day when more than 3,000 of us will call in sick. That would be a last resort. We wouldn't want to do that, but we have to do something.'[85]

While not immediately covered by the *Trade Union Act*, as Ryanair is largely within the jurisdiction of the Irish courts where prohibition of union membership is allowed, this dispute raises some relevant issues for considering trade union organisation and industrial action more generally in the UK. Firstly, the tensions and grievances underlying even latent conflict may have deep roots, beginning their gestation years – perhaps decades – before thus making them difficult to pinpoint. Second, the conflict might range across a large number of geographically spread workplaces, maybe covered by different regulations. Thirdly, the dispute tends to develop through an escalation of exchanges between management and their employees. In this case it is clear that Ryanair refused to engage with either pilots or cabin crew because of an autocratic – 'master and servant' – attitude towards staff, an attitude they were ultimately forced to change. Fourth, it is unclear where or when this escalated into industrial action: there is no definable organised or spontaneous 'walk-out' of staff. And fifthly, what organisation and action that had occurred was via social media, perhaps founded in networks established at work bases. This method replaced mass meetings and large-scale collective engagement. Social media was the basis of the largest unofficial action of recent years, when used during the construction engineers dispute impacting sites in Scotland and the North East of England in 2009.[86] It was, principally, this dispute which led to the coalition government under Cameron establishing the Carr review into the use of 'leverage tactics' by trade unions, which itself was used as a major justification for Cameron, as Prime Minister in the succeeding Conservative government, introducing the *Trade Union Act*.

A revival of trade unionism?

It may be that after decades of declining membership, with trade unions seemingly in their death throes, and predictions that the strike was about to disappear, we might see some sign of renewal. Official figures, on trade union membership and strikes, give no indication for such a view as they still record historic lows. However, it would have been an astute analyst, rather than an optimistic supporter, who could have predicted a revival in the Labour Party after the 2015 election.

Some sign of revival might be seen in the ability, still limited, of unions to recruit and mobilise workers in insecure employment, particularly from migrant communities. There are also grounds for some speculation that this unionisation might spread. Firstly, the solution for poor terms and conditions in the labour market most commonly adopted, of attempting to change job, might have become increasingly exhausted in a general race to the bottom in working conditions. It certainly could be argued that casualisation, agency work, and general precarious employment has moved from the periphery to the core of the labour market. Rather than improving work, such a strategy might have become counterproductive, especially when it has become more difficult to get job seeker benefits. These changes go along with the reform of a benefit system which is designed to make applying so difficult that it drives people into work, comparable to the old workhouse system designed to discourage anyone entering if there was any alternative. But it also encourages low paying employers through in-work benefit; a system of 'making work pay.' Second, there are implications from a collapse of the neoliberal project. The drift from one minimum wage job to another, especially as it advances into later life with increasing living costs may begin to fray. The hold of the common-sense assumptions on individual reliance, rather than collectivism, may also be in the process of collapse. Support of Corbynism in the shift of Labour towards collective values could easily lead to a groundswell of support for unionisation, especially for the current 'new unionism' which has focussed on areas of contract work and bogus self-employment. At the end of the 19th and beginning of the 20th century, new unionism grew rapidly amongst the immigrant, and the casually employed dockers of London and elsewhere. Such could be the same in the early 21st century.

For any prediction of the impact of the *Trade Union Act*, we also need to examine the possible action of the courts and legal system. In the end it will be the interpretation of the Act and rulings by judges which will

Box 4.4 The next Labour government will transform the workplace

The next Labour government will bring in a 20 point plan for security and equality at work:

• Give all workers equal rights from day one, whether part-time or full-time, temporary or permanent – so that all workers have the same rights and protections whatever kind of job they have
• Ban zero hours contracts – so that every worker gets a guaranteed number of hours each week
• Ensure that any employer wishing to recruit labour from abroad does not undercut workers at home - because it causes divisions when one workforce is used against another
• Repeal the Trade Union Act and roll out sectoral collective bargaining – because the most effective way to maintain good rights at work is through a trade union
• Guarantee trade unions a right to access workplaces – so that unions can speak to members and potential members
• Introduce four new Bank Holidays – we'll bring our country together with new holidays to mark our four national patron saints' days, so that workers in Britain get the same proper breaks as in other countries.
• Raise the minimum wage to the level of the living wage (expected to be at least £10 per hour by 2020) – so that no one in work gets poverty pay
• End the public sector pay cap – because public sector wages have fallen and our public sector workers deserve a pay rise
• Amend the takeover code to ensure every takeover proposal has a clear plan in place to protect workers and pensioners – because workers shouldn't suffer when a company is sold
• Roll out maximum pay ratios – of 20:1 in the public sector and companies bidding for public contracts - because it cannot be right that wages at the top keep rising while everyone else's stagnates
• Ban unpaid internships – because it's not fair for some to get a leg up when others can't afford to
• Enforce all workers' rights to trade union representation at work – so that all workers can be supported when negotiating with their employer

- Abolish employment tribunal fees – so that people have access to justice
- Double paid paternity leave to four weeks and increase paternity pay – because fathers are parents too and deserve to spend more time with their new babies
- Strengthen protections for women against unfair redundancy – because no one should be penalised for having children
- Hold a public inquiry into blacklisting – to ensure that blacklisting truly becomes and remains a thing of the past
- Give equalities reps statutory rights – so they have time to protect workers from discrimination
- Reinstate protection against third party harassment – because everyone deserves to be safe at work
- Use public spending power to drive up standards, including only awarding public contracts to companies which recognise trade unions
- Introduce a civil enforcement system to ensure compliance with gender pay auditing– so that all workers have fair access to employment and promotion opportunities and are treated fairly at work

Available from http://press.labour.org.uk/post/160128951404/the-next-labour-government-will-transform-the.

give substance to the requirements on industrial action ballots, the required thresholds, and other aspects of the Act. How will judges rule on injunctions brought on the statement of the cause of dispute, or other issues that may be contested? There is also the issue of workers' rights which will arise after Brexit. While the Conservative government has said that these rights will be carried through into UK law it is certain that any potential changes to: rights of equality; health and safety; working time; employee voice; and much more based on EU Directives, might be challenged in the UK courts.[87] While traditionally, and probably correctly, trade unionists have tended to see the courts as antagonistic territory, partisan towards employers and organised capitalism, a slightly different picture might be drawn from some recent rulings. We have already seen that on two key areas of the Act, on the requirement for a

summary of the issues in dispute to be included on the ballot paper and for dates for industrial action to be specified, have both had rulings sympathetic to the union view.

In early 2017 a Ministry of Justice review of employment tribunal fees was published. Fees were introduced by the coalition government in 2013, with the intention of cutting what they claimed to be 'weak' and 'vexatious' cases brought by malicious employees against their – mostly past – employer hoping for a large pay-out. Arguing this indicated the success of the fees, the review pointed to a decline in cases brought to tribunal by almost 70%. The Supreme Court took a very different view of the decline in cases to tribunals. In a case brought by Unison in July 2017, the Supreme Court argued that the fees 'bear no direct relation to the amount sought and can therefore be expected to act as a deterrent to claims for modest amounts or non-monetary remedies (which together form the majority of ET claims).' They therefore ruled that the 'Fees Order is unlawful under both domestic and EU law because it has the effect of preventing access to justice. Since it had that effect as soon as it was made, it was therefore unlawful and must be quashed.'[88] Fees were not only scrapped but all those who had paid up to £1,200 to bring a case should be reimbursed, a total of more than £27 million.[89] Much of this would be returned to trade unions who, themselves, had taken cases representing members through to tribunal. Those not recompensed were those who couldn't take cases of discrimination, unfair dismissal, unauthorised deduction, redundancy, or other breach of their employment contract because of the fees.

The scrapping of tribunal fees meant an increase in cases. One effect was that it exposed tensions amongst those whose role was to alleviate workplace disputes. Themselves subject to job cuts, as government employees under austerity measures, Acas conciliators act as the initial agents in trying to get reconciliation in tribunal applications. The body which had acted to bring together parties in disputes, most recently in the Royal Mail and in the University disputes, as well as in many others, now faced its own dispute. Faced with a dramatic rise in their workload, Acas conciliators, members of PCS, where in dispute. Following a tribunal ruling in support of the union in early 2018, requiring Acas to consult on changes to conciliators work and grading,[90] the conciliators voted in favour of industrial action.[91]

The Public and Civil Service Union (PCS) was also able to quash a government attempt to make cuts to their redundancy scheme. In anticipation of major cuts in the civil service the Minister responsible announced new terms to the redundancy scheme, terms which represented a 30% cut to payments. A judicial review at the High Court ruled that the government had failed to consult the unions and that they should return to the previous, more generous, redundancy terms agreed between government and unions only six years before. The Court also refused the government right to appeal, making them liable for costs.[92] However, the government has not failed in all its recent cases. Prison Officers, banned from strike action, staged prison gate protests and a withdrawal from voluntary duties in a dispute around pay and conditions around increasing violence in UK prisons. The government gained an injunction to include all these actions in a permanent ban on industrial action.[93]

Unions were successful in legal action against local government. In a dispute with Birmingham City Council, the court awarded Unite a temporary injunction to stop redundancy or downgrading of conditions of the bin collectors. The dispute could be traced back about five years and an equal pay award to women workers for the council amounting to about £1.1 billion. This was resolved by the council by withdrawing bonuses and other extra payments to predominantly male street cleaners and rubbish collectors who had been the comparator in the claim. The latest phase of the conflict revolved around the council attempt to introduce driver control over safety, making 122 safety supervisors for the rear of the vehicles redundant. One of the strikers wrote in the *Guardian* that this was just the latest in the decline of their pay:

'Over the years, we've seen a greater use of workers on insecure zero-hours agency contracts and in 2011 the council cut the number on a wagon from five down to three. Our pay has plummeted in real terms, too. This is also the case for other colleagues at the council. So much so, I've heard of people who have remortgaged their home to help make ends meet. (adding that) The council has said the latest cost-cutting exercise is about working practices and that no one will be made redundant. That, excuse the pun, is rubbish. I'm a grade three and if I want to keep my job in the refuse service I'll have to take a pay cut of £5,000 and be bumped down a grade. That's nearly a 25% pay cut to my £21,000 salary.'[94]

In August, strike action was suspended when the leader of the council and Unite came to an agreement at Acas, where changes to the rubbish collector's hours with a suspension of redundancies was settled. However, the council chief challenged the settlement, arguing that anything which didn't cut pay or continue redundancies was unaffordable, resulting in the resignation of the council leader. Unite then took the matter to the courts to gain the temporary injunction to halt the redundancies. At the time of writing, a full hearing which will decide on who can legitimately make agreements on behalf of the council is still to take place.[95]

The unions have clearly acted to challenge the excesses of government autocratic action, liberating the 'servant' from their arbitrary action. The argument presented by neoliberals, the ideological foundation to all the trade union reforms since the election of the Thatcher government in 1979, are founded not on any attempt at modernisation but designed to return unions to their status in the 19th century. While they deny any inequality of power in the employment contract, the disparity is fundamental. In an economy based on the sale and purchase of people's capacity to work, as a commodity, the whole rationale is one of cheapening the cost of that commodity and the only brake is the seller's capacity to resist the increased exploitation of this ability to work. Just as the unions have managed to act at least as a limited check on government power, and clearly an irritant, so their presence acts as a counter to autocratic employers bent on subordinating workers to a spiralling downwards of employment conditions. It is no coincidence that this race to the bottom in working and employment conditions, the growth of precarious labour, has coincided with the kettling of the unions.

But, while it is necessary to hold the deterioration at bay, there are problems in the unions themselves. Researchers on the impact of the *Trade Union Act*, interviewing union activists and officers, identified four weaknesses in the unions response. First, some unions have become dependent on employers, in part through years of establishing partnership agreements. They have limited relationships with members, in the absence of local and workplace representation. Unions can also become dominated by small clique which is off-putting for new members, however much they might want to be involved. As a one union member told the researchers, 'a [branch officer] who's been steeped in the traditions, is so conversant with the mechanisms and levers of change, that an upstart who might want to come along and make those changes ... can be quickly browbeaten and put in their place'.[96] The trade union movement can also be fragmented and fractious between rival unions. While there has been a considerable reduction, because of merger, the process might sometimes just lead to an internalisation of these tensions.

Repealing the Trade Union Act

In their Manifesto for the 2017 election the Labour Party propose to:

'Repeal the Trade Union Act and roll out sectoral collective bargaining because the most effective way to maintain good rights at work is collectively through a union. Guarantee trade unions a right to access workplaces so that unions can speak to members and potential members.'[97]

Such a shift towards protection for workers is not a particularly radical proposal but would enshrine the protection enjoyed in most industrial countries. A system which protects, and not erodes, the laws and regulation against discrimination, on health and safety, for job protection, and the general comfort and security which has been eroded by governments driven by neoliberal ideology which only protects the interests of employers.

The last Labour government failed to repeal, or even roll back, the 'Thatcher legislation' of the 1980s. Tony Blair famously wanted to leave intact the 'most restrictive' trade union legislation in the western world.[98] Opposition to the kettling of trade unions did come from employment lawyers through the Institute of Employment Rights, consistently presenting alternatives rooted in voluntarism; the recognition of employment standards through a system of collective bargaining. In substantial proposals made in 1996, perhaps anticipating that the Conservative legislation would be reversed by an incoming Labour government, they argued that:

'The downwards spiral ... can only be reversed by a radical change in policy direction. The adoption of an effective system of labour market regulation is an essential precondition of an economy based on a high rate of innovation, high productivity, high quality in production, and full employment based on decent wages and terms and conditions. What Britain thus needs is a programme of re-regulation of the labour market, designed not only to reverse the trend towards greater social and labour market inequality, but also to promote economic efficiency. It would also serve to end the costly and self-defeating reliance on wage subsidies as a means of alleviating low pay.'[99]

Their efforts, at that time, were misplaced as the Blair government, elected after the publication of these IER proposals, insisted on maintaining the Thatcher legislation. Various attempts have been made to make some reform in the tightening legislation, for instance in the *Trade Union Freedom Bill* proposed as a Private Members Bill by John McDonnell in 2010.

In the wake of the *Trade Union Act*, and with the election of Jeremy Corbyn as leader of the Labour Party, the Institute of Employment Rights launched their *Manifesto for Labour Law*. A summary of their proposals is attached as an appendix to this section, one key proposal being:

> 'to shift the focus of labour law from statutory minimum rights to collective bargaining, allowing workers to organise and negotiate for higher wages and conditions within not only their companies but across entire sectors ... We also recommend that the definition of the legal term 'worker' is reviewed, as currently many people working in the burgeoning so-called 'gig' economy (such as Uber drivers, Deliveroo workers, some agency workers, and people on zero-hours contracts) legally fall outside of the eligibility criteria for basic workers' rights, such as sick pay. By reconsidering how labour law works in the context of the 'gig' economy, we can ensure that companies are not able to simply dodge employment law by misclassifying their workers as 'self-employed' or by hiring them on contracts that offer no security.'[100]

Unlike in 1997 the Labour Party has now adopted the IER proposals as the basis for reform of trade union and employment law (see Box 4.4).

A central tenet of Tony Blair and 'New Labour' was the distancing of the party from Labours traditional links with the trade unions. The party, or at least its leadership, assumed the neoliberal mythology that, not only were the trade unions responsible for Britain's economic ills but that they would remain unelectable if they were seen to be in any way allied to them. But the weakening of the trade unions proved no cure for economic ills. Instead there was no protection against an onslaught on pay and conditions as well as the very security and living standards of increasing numbers of people. This only accelerated as austerity measures made workers pay for the more recent economic crisis, no fault of the unions but of bankers and of finance capital.

Any reestablishment of trade union and employment rights will be a struggle not just to return some power to trade unions, to the ability of working people to collectively extend and defend pay, conditions and rights at work, but also against the myths and ideology which acts to hold the 'servants' of the powerful in their place.

Notes:

1. Rajeev Syal, Peter Walker, and Rowena Mason, 'Len McCluskey: Unions Ready to Defy Law Over Public Sector Pay Cap' *The Guardian,* 12 September 2017.

2. Nick Triggle, 'NHS Pay: Unions Agree Deal for 1.3 Million Staff,' *BBC News,* Wednesday 21 March 2018; Denis Campbell and Heather Stewart, 'Lowest Paid NHS Staff May Receive Pay Rise of Up to 29% in New Deal,' *The Guardian,* Wednesday 21 March 2018.

3. See e.g. Frances Perraudin, 'Rubbish Piles Up in Birmingham As Strike Continue' *The Guardian,* 28 July 2017.

4. Knight, Ken, 2017 *Electronic Balloting Review: The Report of the Independent Review of Electronic Balloting for Industrial Action* Department for Business, Energy and Industrial Strategy. p.2 available at: https://www.gov.uk/government/uploads/system/uploads/attachment_data/file/668942/e-balloting-review-report-sir-ken-knight.pdf

5. Early Day Motion 1027, *Electronic Voting For Industrial Action Ballots,* 6th March 2018 https://www.parliament.uk/edm/2017-19/1027/

6. Certification Officer, *Annual Report 2015-2016* (Certification Officer for Trade Unions and Employers' Associations) p. 2-3

7. *Ibid.*

8. https://www.rec.uk.com/news-and-policy/policy-update/changes-to-the-conduct-regulations

9. The National Assembly for Wales, *Research Briefing Trade Union (Wales) Act 2017: Act Summary* (National Assembly for Wales, Research Services, 2017). p.6

10. Ibid, p.1

11. Rebecca Tuck, ed., *Labour Law Highlights 2017* (London: The Institute of Employment Rights, 2017), p. 4.

12. Ibid, p. 5, and Pinsent Masons Quarterly *Trade Union Briefing for Employers* – Winter 2017, https://www.pinsentmasons.com/ELP/Trade%20Union%20Winter%20Briefing_1.pdf

13. Gregor Gall, *The Trade Union Act 2016: What Has Its Impact Been So Far?* (Glasgow: Jimmy Reid Foundation, 2017).

14. IWGB. University of London Security Officers Union Ballots Members for Strike Action at https://iwgb.org.uk/2017/03/03/university-of-london-security-officers-union-ballots-members-for-strike-action/.

15. ibid, and, Stephen Smellie 'Is Strike Action Over?' *Scottish Labour*

Review (2017) p. 21.

16. Jan Colley and John Aston, 'BA Cabin Crew Lose Legal Bid to Halt Cost-Cutting,' *The Independent.* 19 February 2010

17. Stephen Moyes, 'Air Strike Hope British Airways and the Unite Union Have Held 'encouraging' Talks to End a Cabin Crew Strike,' *The Sun*, 16 September 2017.

18. Rob Davies, 'British Airways Risks Strike Action Over Plans to Curb Pension Benefits,' *The Guardian*, 7 September 2017.

19. See Roger Thomas and Raymond Turner, *Mirror Group Newspapers Plc Investigations Under Sections 432(2) and 442 of the Companies Act 1985* Department of Trade and Industry, 1995.
http://www.dti.gov.uk/cld/mirrorgroup/summary.htm

20. Brian Meechan, 'Steel Pensions Scheme Victim to 'Major Mis-Selling Scandal',' *BBC News*, Thursday 15 February 2018.
http://www.bbc.co.uk/news/business-43060272

21. The 'old' Universities which existed pre-1992 operated the USS while those Universities established after 1992 from Polytechnics and Colleges subscribed to the Teachers Pension Scheme. These Universities, therefore, were not part of the dispute.

22. See, Stephen Mustchin 'Public sector restructuring and the re-regulation of industrial relations: the three-decade project of privatisation, liberalisation and marketisation in Royal Mail' *Industrial Relations Journal* 48:4, 294–309 (2017)

23. Cited in *CWU's Four Pillars Of Security Launched*
http://www.cwunorthwest.org/docs/News2017/CWUsFourPillarsOfSecurityLaunched.html

24. ibid

25. See Harris, 2017, *Mediation in the Difference Between Royal Mail and CWU*, Acas, available at http://www.cwu.org/wp-content/uploads/2017/12/LTB-658.17-Attachment-1-Final-Report-Royal-Mail-and-CWU-Med-29-Nov-2017.pdf.

26. Details of the CWU campaign can be found at, CWU *National Four Pillars & Pay Agreement Briefing*, available from
https://www.cwu.org/news/national-four-pillars-pay-agreement-briefing/.

27. Agenda For Growth, *Stability And Long Term Success: A National Agreement Between Royal Mail Group and the Communication Workers' Union* (2013).

28. CWU *National Four Pillars & Pay Agreement Briefings* particularly #7

29. Ibid, Para 16.

30. CWU National Four Pillars & Pay Agreement Briefings #13
31. ibid
32. Lynette Harris, Mediation in the Difference Between Royal Mail and Cwu (Acas, 2017).
33. Cited by Rajeev Syal, 'Royal Mail Halts 48-Hour Strike After Obtaining High Court Injunction,' The Guardian, 12 October 2017.
34. Lynette Harris, *Mediation in the Difference Between Royal Mail and CWU* Acas, 2017.
35. ibid
36. Ibid, Para 16
37. CWU Bulletin #32
38. CWU Bulletin #33
39. CWU, *CWU Reaches Deal with Royal Mail* (Thursday 1 February 2018); available from https://www.cwu.org/news/cwu-reaches-deal-royal-mail/.
40. https://www.cwu.org/campaign/bt-pensions-and-pay/
41. CWU, *CWU Votes Yes to Pay and Four Pillars Agreement* (Wednesday 28 March 2018); available from https://www.cwu.org/news/cwu-votes-yes-to-pay-and-four-pillars-agreement/.
42. BBC News, University Strike: What's It All About? (Wednesday 21 February 2018); available from http://www.bbc.co.uk/news/education-43140729.
43. *UCU Announces 14 Strike Dates at 61 Universities in Pensions Row*, (Monday 29 January 2018) available from https://www.ucu.org.uk/article/9242/UCU-announces-14-strike-dates-at-61-universities-in-pensions-row.
44. Sally Weale, 'UK University Lecturers Strike Over Pay' *The Guardian*, Wednesday 25 May 2016 and Javier Espinoza, 'University Staff to Strike After Failed Talks As Union Threatens to Boycott Marking of Students' Work,' *The Telegraph*, Monday 23 May 2016
45. Jack Grove, 'The Times Higher Education V-C Pay Survey 2018,' *Times Higher Education Supplement*, Thursday 22 February 2018.
46. Sean Coughlan, University Pension Boss's £82,000 Pay Rise *BBC News*, 22 February 2018 http://www.bbc.co.uk/news/education-43157711
47. UCU, Precarious Education: How Much University Teaching Is Being Delivered By Hourly-Paid Academics? University and College Union, 2018.
48. Ibid p. 5
49. See e.g. Jamie Woodcock, Six Points on the Eve of the UCU Strike

(2018); available from . Also Laura McDonald, 'A Fight, Not a Privilege,' *Red Pepper* 219, April/May 2018.

50. Camilla Turner, 'Students Urged to Join Lecturers on the Picket Lines, Despite Fears That Walk Out Will Harm Exams' *The Telegraph,* Tuesday 20 February 2018

51. Camilla Turner, 'Students Urged to Join Lecturers on the Picket Lines, Despite Fears That Walk Out Will Harm Exams,' *The Telegraph,* Tuesday 20 February 2018.

52. Jamie Woodcock, *Six Points on the Eve of the UCU Strike* (2018); available from https://www.notesfrombelow.org/article/six-points-eve-ucu-strike.

53. Richard Adams, 'Oxford University Backs Down in Pensions Dispute' *The Guardian,* Wednesday 7 March 2018.

54. UCU/UUK, *Agreement Reached Between UCU and UUK Under the Auspices of Acas.* 12 March 2018 http://www.employerspensionsforum.co.uk/sites/default/files/document s/ucu-uuk-agreement-acas-12-march.pdf

55. UUK, *Joint Expert Panel Proposed* (Friday 23 March 2018); available from http://www.universitiesuk.ac.uk/news/Pages/Joint-Expert-Panel-Proposed.aspx.

56. Debate on the issues can be found in the series of USSbriefs published at the time of the ballot, especially Deepa Govindarajan Driver and Kurt Mills, *The UUK Offer: Context and Analysis* USS Brief 14, 2018. https://medium.com/ussbriefs/the-uuk-offer-context-and-analysis-c43d909f3bd9; Martin Paul Eve, *Thoughts on the UUK Offer and Why I Voted Yes.* 5 April 2018 https://www.martineve.com/2018/04/05/thoughts-on-the-UUK-offer/; Sam Marsh, *Why Which Way to Vote on the Latest UUK Proposal Should Be an Easy Decision.* 3 April 2018 https://medium.com/ussbriefs/why-which-way-to-vote-on-the-latest-uuk-proposal-should-be-an-easy-decision-48e9d3f533cc

57. http://www.unitetheunion.org/news/bmw-workers-announce-eight-24-hour-strikes-over-pension-robbery/ also Alan Tovey, 'BMW's British Staff Suspend Strikes in 'Pensions Robbery' Row,' *The Telegraph,* 17 May 2017.; Thomas Haworth, 'Strike Again and the Deal Is Off, BMW Workers Told,' Swindon Advertiser, 28 June 2017.

58. Tim Birkbeck, 'Long Running Pensions Dispute at Awe Sites in Aldermaston and Burghfield Finally Resolved After Months of Industrial Action' *Basingstoke Gazette,* 4 September 2017.

59. ONS, *UK Consumer Price Inflation: May 2017* (London: Office of

National Statistics, 2017). June 2017

60. http://www.unitetheunion.org/news/bank-of-england-staff-to-strike-for-first-time-in-50-years/ also Press Association, 'Bank of England Staff to Strike for First Time in Nearly 40 Years After Talks Fail' *The Guardian*, 31 March 2017.

61. Denis Campbell and Heather Stewart, 'Lowest Paid Nhs Staff May Receive Pay Rise of Up to 29% in New Deal,' *The Guardian*, Wednesday 21 March 2018. https://www.theguardian.com/society/2018/mar/21/nhs-staff-65-pay-rise-deal-backed-by-healthcare-unions; Nick Triggle, 'NHS Pay: Unions Agree Deal for 1.3 Million Staff,' *BBC News*, Wednesday 21 March 2018. http://www.bbc.co.uk/news/health-43481341

62. https://www.pcs.org.uk/london-and-the-south-east/lse-action

63. Michael Savage and Jamie Doward, 'NHS Cuts and Public Sector Pay: Will There Be a 'winter of discontent'?' *The Observer*, 9 September 2017.

64. Cited in, 'Rail Strike Chaos to Go on Into the Autumn as Southern Rail Announce Yet More Walk Outs,' *The Telegraph* 18 August 2017.

65. Mason Boycott-Owen, 'Brixton's Ritzy Cinema Workers to Strike As Pay Row Enters Second Year' *The Guardian*, 23 September 2017

66. ONS, *Labour market economic commentary: September 2017* https://www.ons.gov.uk/employmentandlabourmarket/peopleinwork/employmentandemployeetypes/articles/labourmarketeconomiccommentary/september2017

67. BIS, *The Income of the Self-Employed* (London: Department of Business, Innovation and Skills, 2016).

68. See George Ritzer, *The Mcdonaldization Thesis: Explorations and Extensions* (Sage, 1998).

69. BFAWU, Mcdonalds Workers Take Historic Step in Fight for Fairness! (18August 2017); available from http://www.bfawu.org/blog.

70. Aditya Chakrabortty, 'Poverty, Illness, Homelessness – No Wonder Mcdonald's UK Workers Are Going on Strike,' *The Guardian*, 1 September 2017.

71. Shirebrook Colliery. Derbyshire http://www.dmm.org.uk/pitwork/html/sbrook2.htm

72. Full report of the Committee, Employment practices at Sports Direct available at https://publications.parliament.uk/pa/cm201617/cmselect/cmbis/219/21902.htms

73. Commons Select Committee, Mike Ashley Must Be Accountable for

Sports Direct Working Practices (www.parliament.com, 22 July 2016); available from .

74. Rob Davies, 'Sports Direct Workers Invited to Press Sad or Happy Emoji Clocking in,' *The Guardian*, 1 September 2017.

75. http://www.bbc.co.uk/news/business-37629628

76. https://www.theguardian.com/money/2017/sep/25/addison-lee-wrongly-classed-drivers-as-self-employed-tribunal-rules

77. Mathew Taylor, *Good Work: The Taylor Review of Modern Working Practices* (London: Department for Business, Energy & Industrial Strategy). July 2017

78. https://www.tuc.org.uk/news/tuc-comment-taylor-review

79. Taylor op cit

80. IWGB, Deliveroo Drivers on Strike! (IWGB Couriers and Logistics Branch); available from https://iwgbclb.wordpress.com/2016/08/12/deliveroo-drivers-on-strike/.

81. Jamie Woodcock, '#slaveroo: Deliveroo Drivers Organising in the 'gig Economy'' *Novara Wire*, Wednesday 10 August 2016. http://wire.novaramedia.com/2016/08/slaveroo-deliveroo-drivers-organising-in-the-gig-economy/

82. Cited by Rob Davies, 'Ryanair Staff Brand Company a 'Disgrace' Over Handling of Issues' *The Guardian*, 22 September 2017.

83. RTE, *Ryanair Pilots Continue Campaign to Join Unions* (26 September 2017); available from https://www.rte.ie/news/ireland/2017/0926/907648-ryanair/.

84. RTE, *Ryanair Pilots Continue Campaign to Join Unions* (26 September 2017); available from . See also: Mateusz Maszczynski, Why Would Anyone Want to Work As Cabin Crew for Ryanair? Less Pro's and More Con's: All the Details (23 September 2017); available from http://www.paddleyourownkanoo.com/2017/09/23/anyone-want-work-cabin-crew-ryanair-less-pros-cons-details/.

85. Hugh Morris, 'Ryanair Flight Attendant Lifts the Lid on Startling Working Conditions – and Plans for a Revolt' *The Telegraph*, 29 September 2017.

86. See, e.g. Acas, *Report of an Inquiry into the Circumstances Surrounding the Lindsey Oil Refinery Dispute* (London: Advisory, Conciliation and Arbitration Service, 2009). 16th February 2009 Gregor Gall, 'The Engineering Construction Strikes in Britain, 2009,' *Capital and Class* 36, no. 3 (2012).

87. See TUC, *UK Employment Rights and the EU*; available from https://www.tuc.org.uk/sites/default/files/UKemploymentrightsandtheE

U.pdf.

88. R (On the Application of Unison) (Appellant) V Lord Chancellor (Respondent) [2017] UKSC 51 on Appeal From: [2015] Ewca Civ 935, (2017).

89. IER, *Tribunal Fees Unlawful, Says Supreme Court* (2017); available from http://www.ier.org.uk/news/tribunal-fees-unlawful-says-supreme-court.

90. PCS 'Acas told in court ruling that consultation rules apply to them too', 7 Feb 2018 https://www.pcs.org.uk/news/acas-told-in-court-ruling-that-consultation-rules-apply-to-them-too

91. PCS, Conciliators at Acas Vote for Industrial Action ·(Public and Commercial Services Union, Friday 16 March 2018 2018); available from https://www.pcs.org.uk/aviation-group/latest-news/conciliators-at-acas-vote-for-industrial-action.

92. PCS, *Court Quashes Redundancy Scheme Cuts* (4 August 2017); available from http://www.pcs.org.uk/news/court-quashes-redundancy-scheme-cuts.

93. May Bulman, 'Prison Officers Permanently Banned from Striking After Government Wins High Court Bid,' T*he Independent,* 19 July 2017

94. Anonymous, 'Birmingham Refuse Workers Hate to See Rubbish Piling Up – But Our Strike Is Vital,' *The Guardian,* 5 August 2017.

95. Helen Pidd, 'Birmingham Council Leader Quits Over Handling of Bin Strike' *The Guardian,* 11 September 2017, and Neil Elkes, 'Birmingham's Bin Strike Suspended After Dustmen Win Legal Battle' *Birmingham Mail,* 20 September 2017.

96. Fenella Porter et al., 'Voices From the Movement: What Can the Trade Union Act (2016) Tell Us About Trade Union Organising?' *Renewal* 25, no. 2 (2017).

97. Labour Party, For the Many Not the Few (2017), p. 45; available from http://www.labour.org.uk/page/-/Images/manifesto-2017/Labour%20Manifesto%202017.pdf.

98. Anthony Blair, "We Won't Look Back to the 1970s,"The Times, Monday 31 March 1997 1997.

99. Keith Ewing, ed., Working Life: A New Perspective on Labour Law (London: Institute of Employment Rights and Lawrence & Wishart, 1996), p. 26

100. From http://www.ier.org.uk/manifesto

Appendix 1

Examples of workers who deliver 'important public services' under the 40% threshold

The following information sets out examples of workers who are considered to deliver the specified important public services. It is for trade unions in the first instance to determine which of their members are normally engaged in the provision of the specific services and therefore potentially subject to the 40% threshold.

KEY:
Important public service
Examples of workers who deliver this service

Health
Emergency, urgent or critical healthcare services, including:
Services provided in an emergency by an ambulance or associated transport service, including dealing with calls for help and organising their response
Paramedic, Emergency care assistant, Emergency technician, Emergency dispatcher
Accident and emergency services in a hospital
Doctor, Nurse
Services which are provided in high-dependency units and intensive care in a hospital
Doctor, Nurse
Psychiatric services provided by a hospital for conditions which require immediate attention in order to prevent serious injury, serious illness or loss of life
Psychiatrist, Doctor, Nurse
Obstetric and midwifery services provided by a hospital for conditions which require immediate attention in order to prevent serious injury, serious illness or loss of life
Obstetrician, Midwife, Doctor, Nurse

Education
Teaching and other services provided by teachers and persons appointed to fulfil the role of a head teacher to persons of compulsory school age at a school other than a fee-paying school, a 16-19 Academy or an institution within the further education sector other than one whose services to persons of compulsory school age are not publicly funded

Appendices

Teachers, Those fulfilling the role of a head teacher, including Academy principals

Fire

Fire fighting services, including dealing with calls for help and organising their response

Fire-fighters, Airport fire-fighters, MOD fire-fighters, Fire-fighter managers, Control centre staff, Control centre managers

Transport

Any bus service which is a London local service as defined in section 179(1) of the Greater London Authority Act 1999

Bus drivers, Engineers, Depot managers

Passenger railway services (including metro, underground and tramway services), including maintenance of trains or of the network, signalling or controlling the operation of the network, and other services which enable trains to operate

Station staff - *despatch staff, safety and security staff, and station supervisors*

Train staff - *train drivers, guards and conductors responsible for train despatch, rail engineers and maintenance staff, and management and control staff including train crew and fleet rostering*

Operations staff - *control room staff, signallers and signalling maintained, infrastructure operators, incident and emergency response staff, and network maintenance*

Civil air traffic control services

Licensed air traffic controllers

Airport security services

Airport workers and managers who are directly involved in carrying out the following security activities:

•Controlling access to an area of an airport designated as a critical part

•Screening persons, items or vehicles entering a critical part

•Searching and/or patrolling critical parts

Port security services

Port security officers who are directly involved in canrying the following security activities:

•Controlling access to an area of a portdesignated as a critical part

•Screening persons, items or vehicles entering a critical part

•Searching and/or patrolling critical parts

Designated Port Facility Security Officers (PFSO) at each port facility

Border security

Services related to border control functions in respect of the entry and exit of

people and goods into and from the United Kingdom
Border Force officers of all grades who are directlyengaged in:
• Immigration and customs controls at UK borders. This covers those who are physically present at the border as well as those present where goods are first encountered in the UK.
• Intelligence and targeting functions which directly support immigration and customs controls at UK borders. This covers intelligence officers in both regional and national offices, as well as those in the Watchlist and Information Control Unit and the National Border Targeting Centre.
• Regional and national command and control structures for a critical incident escalation, and who provide mandated authorities on border matters. This covers officers in both regional Command and Control Units and National Operations Command and Control.

Appendix 2

Facilities Time, or time off for trade union duties listed.

Acas, Time Off for Trade Union Duties and Activities: Code of Practice, (London: The Stationary Office, 2010).

The subjects connected with collective bargaining may include one or more of the following:

(a) terms and conditions of employment, or the physical conditions in which workers are required to work. Examples could include:
• pay
• hours of work
• holidays and holiday pay
• sick pay arrangements
• pensions
• learning and training
• equality and diversity
• notice periods
• the working environment
• operation of digital equipment and other machinery;

(b) engagement or non engagement, or termination or suspension of employment or the duties of employment, of one or more workers. Examples

could include:
• recruitment and selection policies
• human resource planning
• redundancy and dismissal arrangements;
• pensions
• learning and training
• equality and diversity
• notice periods
• the working environment
• operation of digital equipment and other machinery;

(c) allocation of work or the duties of employment as between workers or groups of workers. Examples could include:
• job grading
• job evaluation
• job descriptions
• flexible working practices
• work-life balance;

(d) matters of discipline. Examples could include:
•disciplinary procedures
•arrangements for representing or accompanying employees at internal interviews
•arrangements for appearing on behalf of trade union members, or as witnesses, before agreed outside appeal bodies or employment tribunals;

(e)trade union membership or non membership. Examples could include:
•representational arrangements
•any union involvement in the induction of new workers;

(f)facilities for trade union representatives. Examples could include any agreed arrangements for the provision of:
•accommodation
•equipment
•names of new workers to the union;

(g) machinery for negotiation or consultation and other procedures. Examples could include arrangements for:
•collective bargaining at the employer and/or multi-employer level
•grievance procedures

•joint consultation

•communicating with members

•communicating with other union representatives and union full-time officers concerned with collective bargaining with the employer.

Appendix 3

Role of Certification Officer

The Certification Officer will have new powers to investigate and determine breaches of certain statutory provisions without the need for a complaint from a member.

• The Certification Officer will have new powers to impose financial penalties up to £20,000 where an enforcement order is made or where there exists the power to make an enforcement order but one is not made.

• The Certification Officer will have new powers to enforce his or her own orders.

• Appeals from the Certification Officer to the Employment Appeals Tribunal will generally be on a point of fact or law. Presently all such appeals are only on a point of law.

• Trade unions will be under a duty to include significantly more information in their annual returns to the Certification Officer. In particular, trade unions will have to report on:

– all industrial action undertaken by that trade union and all ballots relating to industrial action

– all payments made by that trade union on political purposes and any other payment from its political fund if not made for a political purpose.

• The Certification Officer will have new powers to enforce these reporting requirements by way of declarations, orders and financial penalties.

• The law relating to the way members of trade unions contribute to the political funds of their unions is to be amended to favour a system of opting in rather that requiring members to opt out of making an otherwise automatic contribution. The changes that this will require to the political fund rules of trade unions will need to be approved by the Certification Officer.

• The majority of the costs of running the Certification Office are to be recouped by way of a levy on trade unions and employers' associations. The scheme under which this levy is to operate will be the responsibility of the Certification Officer, subject to further consultation and regulations.

From report *Certification Officer, Annual Report* 2015-2016 (Certification Officer for Trade Unions and Employers' Associations). p.2

Appendix 4
Institute of Employment Rights, Manifesto for Labour Law

Principal Recommendations

1. A new government department - a Ministry of Labour - should be established to represent the interests of workers in government. The Ministry should be led by a Secretary of State with a seat in the Cabinet.

2. It should be a primary responsibility of the Ministry of Labour to promote collective bargaining and do so on a multi-employer sectoral basis, working with ACAS for this purpose.

3. Sectoral collective bargaining should be promoted through Sectoral Employment Commissions, which would operate through Sectoral Collective Agreements, which in turn would apply to all workers in the sector in question.

4. Sectoral collective bargaining should be complemented by enterprise based bargaining between an employer or a group of employers on the one hand and a trade union or trade unions on the other.

5. Where there are overlapping sectoral and enterprise agreements, the principle of favourability will apply so that the worker is entitled to the most favourable terms and conditions.

6. In order to promote enterprise based collective bargaining, the statutory recognition procedure should be revised so that a union is entitled to recognition if it can show 10% membership and evidence of majority support.

7. Every worker should be entitled to be represented by a trade union collectively or individually on all matters relating to employment, and the statutory right to be accompanied by a trade union official should be amended accordingly.

8. The balance of regulating terms and conditions of employment should in these ways return from the current focus on legislation to a greater focus on collective bargaining, with the clear aim of raising collective bargaining density.

9. There would nevertheless continue to be a role for regulatory legislation to underpin collective bargaining on a range of matters such as pay, working time (including zero hours contracts), discrimination, equality, and health and safety at work.

10. Existing statutory standards should be comprehensively reviewed, and the Low Pay Commission should be renamed the Living Wage Commission: the object is to eliminate rather than entrench low pay.

11. Existing statutory standards should be universal in scope and effective in application. The legal definition of a worker should be greatly expanded and the Tory led changes (including fees) to the employment tribunals reversed.

12. Steps should be taken to resolve more disputes without recourse to the law, under collectively agreed procedures, or summarily by labour inspectors with powers to cancel dismissal notices and order reinstatement.

13. The law on freedom of association should be changed to strike a better balance between trade union autonomy and trade union democracy. Trade union elections should be conducted in accordance with trade union rules and procedures.

14. More effective legislation should be introduced to stamp out blacklisting, which should be regarded as an aggravated breach of labour market regulation, and attract criminal penalties (including imprisonment).

15. It should not be lawful to dismiss a workplace representative except for good cause, requiring the prior approval of a senior labour inspector, whose decision would be subject to review at the instance of the agrieved party by an employment tribunal.

16. Recognised or representative trade unions should have the right to check off facilities on request, and the reserve powers of ministers relating to facilities introduced by the Trade Union Act 2016 should be repealed.

17. The role of the Certification Officer should revert to the jurisdiction at the time the Trade Union Act 2016 was introduced. The investigatory powers introduced by the Trade Union Act 2016 should be removed.

18. The Certification Officer should be required to certify that union industrial action rules conform to basic statutory principles so as to secure a fair, free, and secret ballot, supervised by an independent scrutineer.

19. It should be lawful for everyone to be able to take collective action with others in defence of their social and economic interests in the workplace, and for their trade unions to organise such action.

20. It must be permissible for trade unions to take or to call for industrial action in support of any other workers in dispute (including industrial action involving another employer) where the primary action is lawful.

21. Those participating in lawful collective action must be reinstated at the end of the strike, if it is their wish to be reinstated. The restrictions on agencies supplying strike-breakers should be retained.

22. An injunction should be available on the ground only that the employer could satisfy the court that on the apparent facts the action of the union was unlawful. This should be stated expressly to apply 'notwithstanding any EU law to the contrary'.

23. There should be no legal distinction drawn between public and private sector disputes. Where appropriate it will continue to be possible for unions voluntarily to conclude minimum service agreements in essential services.

24. A Labour Court should be established, with specialist judges. The ET, CAC

and CO should be the first tier of an autonomous Labour Court system with exclusive jurisdiction to deal with all employment and labour related matters.

25. The Trade Union Act 2016 should be repealed in its entirety, immediately.

Acknowledgments

This book arose from the campaign against the *Trade Union Bill 2015*. Tom Unterrainer suggested that a short guide to the measures introduced be expanded into a book explaining the Act. Tom not only suggested the book, but also acted as editor. I would also like to thank Jeremé Snook and Paul Wilkinson who gave expert comment on earlier drafts, to Angie Mindel for correcting my spelling and punctuation as well as comments on the text at all stages, to Louis Tuckman for the cover design, and, in particular, to Mark Serwotka for writing the foreword and to the Public and Commercial and Services Union for their generous support.

About the Author

Alan Tuckman is an Honorary Fellow at the University of Keele and is one of the founders of workerscontrol.net, a multinlingual knowledge base maintained by an international network of activists and academics with both theoretical insight and hands-on experience on issues of workers' self-management and company recuperation.

Kettling the Unions?

Social Media Resource

Search FaceBook for 'Kettling the Unions?'.

For the latest updates, news and commentary on anti-union laws, the *Trade Union Act*, industrial action and more.